1978

# VIRGINIA WOOLF'S MRS. DALLOWAY

## A STUDY IN ALIENATION

# TEXT AND CONTEXT

*Editors*

**ARNOLD KETTLE**
Professor of Literature
Open University

*and*

**A. K. THORLBY**
Professor of Comparative Literature
University of Sussex

◆

*Other Titles in Preparation*

# VIRGINIA WOOLF'S MRS DALLOWAY

## A STUDY IN ALIENATION

### Jeremy Hawthorn

SUSSEX UNIVERSITY PRESS

1975

Published for

SUSSEX UNIVERSITY PRESS

BY

Chatto & Windus Ltd
40 William IV Street
London WC2N 4DF

*

Clarke, Irwin & Co Ltd
Toronto

Hardback ISBN 0 85621 046 3
Paperback ISBN 0 85621 047 1
© Jeremy Hawthorn 1975
Printed in Great Britain by
Cox & Wyman Ltd
London, Fakenham and Reading

# CONTENTS

# ACKNOWLEDGEMENTS

I wish to express my appreciation of the debt I owe to my editors, whose sympathetic but scrupulous help has been invaluable in the writing of this book, and to my colleagues in general and Bill Scott in particular, from whom many valuable insights have come.

My thanks are also due to the staff of the Library of Sheffield Polytechnic, without whose efficiency and co-operation this book would have taken much longer to write.

Acknowledgements are due to The Hogarth Press, Harcourt Brace Jovanovich Inc., for permission to reproduce copyright extracts from the following works: *A Room of One's Own*, *A Writer's Diary*, *Collected Essays*, volumes 1, 2 and 4, *Jacob's Room*, *Mrs. Dalloway*, *Mrs. Dalloway's Party* (edited by Stella McNichol), *Night and Day*, by Virginia Woolf; *Beginning Again*, by Leonard Woolf; and *Virginia Woolf A Biography* (volumes I and II) by Quentin Bell.

# NOTE ON ABBREVIATIONS

AROOO    Virginia Woolf, *A Room of One's Own* (The Hogarth Press, London, Uniform Edition), 14th impression, 1967.

AWD    Virginia Woolf, *A Writer's Diary*, ed. Leonard Woolf (The Hogarth Press, London), 6th impression, 1972.

BA    Leonard Woolf, *Beginning Again* (The Hogarth Press, London), 1964.

CE1/2/4    Virginia Woolf, *Collected Essays*, Volumes 1, 2 and 4 (The Hogarth Press, London), 1966, 1966, 1967.

DS    R. D. Laing, *The Divided Self* (Penguin Books, Harmondsworth), 1970.

EPM    Karl Marx, *Economic and Philosophical Manuscripts of 1844*, trans. M. Milligan (Lawrence and Wishart, London), 1970.

JR    Virginia Woolf *Jacob's Room* (The Hogarth Press, London, Uniform Edition), 10th impression, 1965.

MD    Virginia Woolf, *Mrs. Dalloway* (The Hogarth Press, London, Uniform Edition), 12th impression, 1968.

        NOTE: page references for this edition vary no more than two pages from page references to the Penguin edition which has a total of two more pages than The Hogarth Press edition.

MDP    Virginia Woolf, *Mrs. Dalloway's Party A Short Story Sequence*, ed. Stella McNichol (The Hogarth Press, London), 1973.

NAD    Virginia Woolf, *Night and Day* (The Hogarth Press, London, Uniform Edition) 8th impression, 1966.

VWA B1/2    Quentin Bell, *Virginia Woolf A Biography*, Volumes I and II (The Hogarth Press, London), 1972.

# I

# TOGETHER AND APART

Mrs Dalloway said she would buy the flowers herself.

'I will come,' said Peter, but he sat on for a moment. What is this terror? what is this ecstasy? he thought to himself. What is it that fills me with extraordinary excitement?
It is Clarissa, he said.
For there she was.

(MD pp. 5, 213.)

In between the 'Mrs Dalloway' of the first line of Virginia Woolf's novel, and the 'Clarissa' of the concluding lines of its last page, the reader is led to an awareness of the enormous complexity of the character in question. On a simple level we can say that we move from a view of 'Mrs Dalloway' – the married woman bearing her husband's name and thus seen in terms of her relationship with other people – to 'Clarissa', a person in her own right. But this ignores the fact that the final, extraordinarily striking, view of Clarissa's 'full selfhood' is achieved through the eyes of another person, Peter Walsh. It is also worth noting that although this powerful perception of Clarissa's human distinctness is presented in terms of an epiphany, a sudden illumination, the progression through the tenses (I will come, It is Clarissa, For there she was), suggests that this view of her full selfhood that Peter Walsh obtains is dependent upon a knowledge of Clarissa's existence over time, from the days of his acquaintance with her at Bourton to the contact with her which he knows is to come after her party.

*Mrs. Dalloway*, I would argue, is an extended investigation of the paradoxes contained implicitly in the opening and closing lines of the novel. Clarissa Dalloway is seen as an individual whose identity varies according to the situation in which she finds herself; at different times, and with different people, she appears to be a different person. And yet 'there she was'. Along with Peter Walsh, the reader feels that in spite of the multiple, even contradictory, aspects of her personality which are revealed to him, Clarissa Dalloway is *there*, distinct, unique. In the pages

9

that follow I want to suggest that there were – and are – particular reasons why this paradoxical nature of human identity should have fascinated Virginia Woolf so much, and that these are connected with the social phenomenon which we call alienation.

We generally assume that although different people may have different, and contradictory, views of us, we ourselves have some conception of the integrity and unity of our own personalities. It is true that different characters (not to mention critics) see Clarissa Dalloway in very different ways. But it is not true that she herself has a clear conception of any well-defined self of which she is possessed. She distinguishes between selves appropriate, it appears, to different social circumstances:

> . . . this being Mrs Dalloway; not even Clarissa any more; this being Mrs Richard Dalloway.
> *(MD* p. 13)

and she seems to see within her self aspects of her youth and her maturity which do not necessarily combine to produce a unified or unambiguous identity:

> She would not say of any one in the world now that they were this or were that. She felt very young; at the same time unspeakably aged.
> *(MD* p. 10)

And yet Peter Walsh feels that 'there she was', that he has an insight into her which is somehow complete, which *does* say that she is 'this or that'.

Looking at her own reflection in the mirror, Clarissa sees:

> . . . the delicate pink face of the woman who was that very night to give a party; of Clarissa Dalloway; of herself.
>
> How many million times she had seen her face, and always with the same imperceptible contraction! She pursed her lips when she looked in the glass. It was to give her face point. That was her self – pointed; dart-like; definite. That was her self when some effort, some call on her to be her self, drew the parts together, she alone knew how different, how incompatible and composed so for the world only into one centre, one diamond, one woman who sat in her drawing-room and made a meeting-point . . .
> *(MD* p. 42)

It is worth noting the distinction between 'herself' and 'her self' that this passage presents us with – a distinction, incidentally, obscured in the Penguin edition of *Mrs. Dalloway*, which alters 'her self' to 'herself'. The distinction is important, because although Clarissa seems able to use the term 'herself' without quibble, the term 'her self', which suggests something much more  fixed and distinct, is something that she sees as artificial, produced only for other people. It is in fact another person – Peter Walsh – who, at the end of the novel, perceives Clarissa's distinct self. Clarissa, on the other hand, thinks that she is composed of incompatible parts, and the connotations of artificiality brought to mind by the word 'composed' are focused more sharply by the diamond image, calling to mind artificiality and the Philistine display of wealth, as well as a certain hardness not suggestive of the sympathetically human.

The image of the diamond is an ambiguous one, and in its ambiguity we see the central paradox of human personality with which Virginia Woolf is attempting to grapple. Immediately before the 'composing' passage the diamond image is associated with the kiss given to the youthful Clarissa by Sally Seton – a moment of purity and integrity. But the single person that Clarissa 'assembles' on the landing before descending is seen as 'that diamond shape', and here it is an artificiality that seems to be being stressed. Perhaps most striking is a much later description of Lady Bruton, in which certain distinct echoes from the 'composing' passage can be detected. For the sinister Lady Bruton, emigration (her pet obsession), has become an object:

> . . . round which the essence of her soul is daily secreted [and] becomes inevitably prismatic, lustrous, half looking-glass, half precious stone; now carefully hidden in case people should sneer at it; now proudly displayed.
>
> (*MD* p. 120)

In Lady Bruton we see fully developed those negative aspects of the 'diamond' aspect of Clarissa: hard, self-regarding, artificial and unamenable to real human contact and mutual adaptation.

'Together and Apart' is the title of one of Virginia Woolf's short stories which is concerned with the same central paradox to which I have already made reference in talking about *Mrs.*

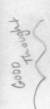

*Dalloway.* Virginia Woolf seems to be fascinated by the fact that a human being's distinctness only reveals itself through contact with other people, and can only be fully perceived by another person. We exist simultaneously in terms of but distinct from other people – together with and apart from them. Thus on the one hand Clarissa can feel that Peter Walsh 'made her see herself', and that:

> . . . to know her, or any one, one must seek out the people who completed them; even the places. . . . [and] since our apparitions, the part of us which appears, are so momentary compared with the other, the unseen part of us, which spreads wide, the unseen might survive, be recovered somehow attached to this person or that, or even haunting certain places, after death.
>
> (*MD* p. 168)

But on the other hand the novel suggests, paradoxically, that human beings are possessed of a central irreducible core of identity, which exists independently of other people. Throughout the novel the words 'self' and 'soul' are used to suggest this irreducible centre.

In her diary Virginia Woolf commented on the 'peculiar repulsiveness of those who dabble their fingers self approvingly in the stuff of others' souls', and in spite of the expressed belief of Clarissa's that to know her one must search out the people who completed her, *Mrs. Dalloway* also insists on the importance of a respect for the privacy of the soul. Sir William Bradshaw wants to dabble his fingers in Septimus's soul: he is introduced, ironically we feel, as one who has 'understanding of the human soul', but Clarissa feels that he is capable of 'forcing your soul'. Miss Kilman's desire to subdue Clarissa's soul and its mockery is likewise seen as an inexcusable desire to intrude into the privacy of another person's inner-self.

Again, we come face to face with a paradox. The soul is private, and must not be 'forced', but it can be destroyed by being made *too* private, by too much protection. We know that Peter Walsh talked to Clarissa about the defects of her soul at Bourton, and he associates the death of her soul with her symbolic rejection of sexuality when she left the table in confusion in response to Sally Seton's 'daring' remark. Sallly, on

12

the other hand, feared that the Hughs and the Dalloways and all the other perfect gentlemen would stifle Clarissa's soul. When Dr Holmes bursts into Septimus's room he is involved in a symbolic action similar to Peter Walsh's bursting in on Clarissa; both are guilty, in different ways, of wanting to force the soul of another person. Septimus kills himself rather than surrender the privacy of his soul, and Clarissa rejects Peter Walsh, for:

> . . . with Peter everything had to be shared; everything gone into. And it was intolerable, and when it came to that scene in the little garden by the fountain, she had to break with him or they would have been destroyed, both of them ruined. . . .
>
> (*MD* p. 10)

Yet in attempting to preserve that necessary privacy Clarissa may, the reader suspects, have stifled her own soul. Unlike Peter, who at one point in the novel comes to the conclusion that he no longer needs people, Clarissa needs her privacy to be tempered with human contact:

> She had a sense of comedy that was really exquisite, but she needed people, always people, to bring it out . . .
>
> (*MD* p. 87)

In cutting herself off from Peter, we feel that she may have cut herself off from a necessary contact with others. Thus when Richard leaves her to lunch with Lady Bruton, she feels of Peter that:

> . . . If I had married him, this gaiety would have been mine all day!
>
> It was all over for her. The sheet was stretched and the bed narrow. . . . Richard, Richard! she cried, as a sleeper in the night starts and stretches a hand in the dark for help. Lunching with Lady Bruton, it came back to her. He has left me; I am alone for ever, she thought, folding her hands upon her knee.
>
> (*MD* pp. 52, 53)

A parallel scene to this describes Septimus's feeling of terror at being left alone when Rezia leaves him, immediately before

13

his suicide. Both characters – although on different levels – need other people whilst fearing the threat to their privacy that contact with others involves.

How is such a paradoxical combination of needs to be reconciled? One way of reconciling two contradictory or apparently irreconcilable pressures is to alternate between them. It would appear that in a number of different areas this alternation between irreconcilables presented itself to Virginia Woolf as the most effective solution to various problems. In her essay 'Life and the Novelist', she writes that:

*proportle* [The novelist] must expose himself to life . . . But at a certain moment he must leave the company and withdraw, alone . . .

(*CE2* p. 136)

Clarissa, like the novelist, feels the need both to expose herself to life, and to withdraw, alone. Her party is, for her, an exposure, but in the middle of it she feels the need to withdraw alone to the privacy of her room.

Thinking about Clarissa's party, Peter Walsh comes to a conclusion about the nature of the soul:

For this is the truth about our soul, he thought, our self, who fish-like inhabits deep seas and plies among obscurities threading her way between the boles of giant weeds, over sun-flickered spaces and on and on into gloom, cold, deep, inscrutable; suddenly she shoots to the surface and sports on the wind-wrinkled waves; that is, has a positive need to brush, scrape, kindle herself, gossiping.

(*MD* p. 177)

So Peter Walsh's earlier belief that he no longer needs people has to be qualified. It is interesting to compare this passage with a passage from R. D. Laing's *The Divided Self*, describing the life-style of one of Laing's schizophrenic patients:

. . . he maintained himself in isolated detachment from the world for months, living alone in a single room, existing frugally on a few savings, day-dreaming. But in doing this, he began to feel he was dying inside; he was becoming more and more empty, and observed 'a progressive impoverishment of my life mode'. A great deal of his pride and self-

14

esteem was implicated in thus existing on his own, but as his state of depersonalization progressed he would emerge into social life for a brief foray in order to get a 'dose' of other people, but 'not an overdose'.

(*DS* p. 53)

I will argue in chapter three that what Virginia Woolf referred to as her 'madness' seems to have presented her with experiences which, in a sense, can be seen as exaggerated versions of 'normal' social experiences. Only in a sense, however, for they are normal only in the context of certain specific social situations. The alternation forced upon Laing's patient, Woolf's 'novelist', and Clarissa, is one that becomes necessary only when the individual feels that life makes demands upon him which are contradictory but which cannot be evaded. One critic has a fertile suggestion to make concerning the nature of the different attitudes towards Clarissa held by those who know her:

> The other characters' fragmentary glimpses of Mrs Dalloway exist side by side, each contradicted but uncancelled by the others, all of them together suggesting the total incompatible aspects of her personality of which only she is aware.[1]

The phrase 'contradicted but uncancelled' reminds us that *Mrs. Dalloway*, unlike the 'classical novel' of the nineteenth century,[2] presents the reader with no moral or other overview within which all contradictions can be subsumed, or by reference to which all conflicts can be resolved.

Clarissa leads a life that is full of contradictions, and so her self too is lacking in consistency. Now it is arguable that in *any* social situation men and women will have both public and private lives. What needs to be added to this assertion is that the extent of the privacy that men and women need will vary from situation to situation, and that the existence of contradictions between these different aspects of a single life is by no means universal. To put the argument the other way round, it seems hard to deny that one of the characteristics of capitalist society is that the distinction between public and private lives is magnified, and that there is a qualitative change from a *distinction* to a *contradiction* between the two. Clarissa is forced to be one person in one situation, and another person in a different situation, because there are fundamental contradictions

15

in the society of which she is a part and in the human relationships which constitute it. Any search for the 'real' Clarissa on the part of either the reader, or of a character such as Peter Walsh, is thus doomed to failure. Peter Walsh's Clarissa is different from Richard Dalloway's Clarissa. Clarissa herself would like to 'compose' a unified and consistent self. The question that she has to answer before she does this, however, is the question that is posed explicitly in the novel on a number of occasions: 'to whom?'. Peter, Richard, Sally?...

The movement from the 'classical' to the 'modernist' novel can, at the risk of indulging in over-large generalisations, be compared to the movement from classical to quantum physics. In both cases we have a movement from the presentation of facts which could be reconciled with one another by reference to a single, unified body of truth (the laws of classical physics or the moral overview of the classical novel, both of which were presented as if they existed independently of the observer who perceived them), towards a situation where evidence is presented which cannot be 'fitted together' by reference to some overriding absolute or set of absolutes. The phrase 'contradicted but uncancelled' is strikingly similar to a comment by the physicist Niels Bohr, in an article dealing with the problem of reconciling information about a number of objects produced by experiments based on different, and apparently irreconcilable, scientific premisses:

> . . . evidence obtained under different experimental conditions cannot be comprehended within a single picture, but must be regarded as *complementary* in the sense that only the totality of the phenomena exhausts the possible information about the objects.[8]

Isn't that last phrase applicable to our knowledge of Clarissa Dalloway? We cannot work out what she is like, what she *is*, merely by studying what she thinks of herself, or what Peter Walsh, or Richard Dalloway, or Doris Kilman think of her. She *is* all these things, and only her whole life, including all her thoughts about herself and her relationships with other people, exhausts the possible information about her.

Clarissa's great moral strength comes from her attempt – in her party – to draw people out of their isolation in much the

16

same way as she draws the folds of her dress together with her needle. In her famous essay 'Modern Fiction', Virginia Woolf wrote that the novelist was able to put himself at any point of view, or even, to some extent, to combine different views. Her early manuscript notes for *Mrs. Dalloway* include the aim of giving two points of view at once[4] (an aim that many different artists, working in different art forms, seem to have shared in the early part of the present century). Certainly the whole novel seems to be trying to connect and combine (but not necessarily to reconcile) different and contradictory views of Clarissa, which seem to be related to contradictions in Clarissa herself which are, in part at least, the product of a divided society.

## 2

# OYSTER AND SHELL

In her essay 'Mr. Bennett and Mrs. Brown' Virginia Woolf noted that a convention in writing was not much different from a convention in manners, and that both in life and literature it was necessary to have some means of bridging the gap between the hostess and her unknown guest – or the writer and his unknown reader. She further noted that

> At the present moment we are suffering, not from decay, but from having no code of manners which writers and readers accept as a prelude to the more exciting intercourse of friendship.
>
> (*CE1* p. 334)

'Mr. Bennett and Mrs. Brown' was read as a paper to the Heretics at Cambridge eight days before she wrote in her diary that her mind was full of *The Hours* – later to be retitled *Mrs. Dalloway*. It is thus arguable that the practical problems she was encountering in the composition of her novel inform the theoretical discussion in the essay, and in an unusually complex way. On one level Virginia Woolf is obviously concerned with the problem of communicating with her future reader, with finding some common code which will allow communication to take place. But the use of the party metaphor in the essay – witness her comparison of the writer–reader relationship to the hostess–guest relationship – suggests that she is aware of important parallels between her problems of communicating as a writer, and her characters' problems of communicating as people.

The novelist who wishes to concern himself with an examination of, say, violence, is not presented with the same sort of problem as faces the novelist concerned to write about human privacy and alienation. Violence is public and observable and involves some form of communication between human beings. The novelist's task is thus – if I may oversimplify – to translate one form of contact into another. Human privacy is by definition something that is *not* communicated – at least not directly

– and so the novelist who wishes to convey the experience of privacy and alienation to his reader has to find a 'code', as Virginia Woolf expresses it, where none exists in everyday life. The novel seeks to give a public significance to those matters it treats of, and thus there is a central paradox involved in the novel which has as its subject matter the incommunicable – a paradox which has become familiar to us in the course of the twentieth century. It is worth pondering the skill with which a writer such as Beckett communicates the absence of communication between his characters.

It has been suggested that Virginia Woolf's words seem to be controlled more by the impulses of a literary convention than by the need to capture a special and peculiar experience.[5] I think that this view is mistaken, and it is one that was explicitly contradicted by Virginia Woolf herself in the case of *Mrs. Dalloway*. In the *Introduction* she wrote for the 1928 *Modern Library* edition of the novel, she denied that the book was the deliberate offspring of a method, and claimed that it was more the case that, in writing the novel, she became dissatisfied with nature for giving her an idea without providing a house for it to live in:

> Thus rebuked the idea started as the oyster starts or the snail to secrete a house for itself. And this it did without any conscious direction.

In other words, the form of *Mrs. Dalloway* grew out of a desire to communicate something for which no accepted convention of literary communication existed. The novelist may describe solipsistic states, but he cannot *be* both a solipsist and a novelist simultaneously.

I have suggested that there is probably an analogy, certainly a connection, between the problems Virginia Woolf faced in communicating the experience of alienation to her readers, and the problems her alienated characters face in attempting to communicate with one another. In both cases she seems to have seen the need for the discovery of a common 'code of manners', which may suggest why the party performs such an important symbolic function in *Mrs. Dalloway*. I think, however, that it is possible to go further than this and to argue that consciously or unconsciously Virginia Woolf connected the

19

problems of literary and personal communication, and that this is not surprising as many of these spring from common ground. It is worth comparing the quotation above, taken from her 1928 *Introduction* to *Mrs. Dalloway*, with the following quotation which is taken from her essay 'Street Haunting'. In the following passage she is describing the dropping of a public mask, or persona, which is possible when one leaves the privacy of one's own house for the anonymity of the street (an action which, in *Mrs. Dalloway*, gathers a symbolic force suggestive of the journey from public self to private consciousness):

> ... when the door shuts on us, all that vanishes. The shell-like covering which our souls have excreted to house themselves, to make for themselves a shape distinct from others, is broken, and there is left of all these wrinkles and roughnesses a central oyster of perceptiveness, an enormous eye.
>
> (*CE4* p. 156)

Both human beings and novels excrete shells which give them form, distinct shape, and identity. These shells allow the 'inner' to be communicated to the reader, or to other people, without its being dissipated. But the shell must be an appropriate one, it must grow out of the needs of the matter to be communicated, rather than being imposed on it and suffocating it, and it must on occasions be broken and reformed.

Virginia Woolf's problem as a novelist is analogous to the problem of the alienated individual: both wish to communicate an inner-reality rather than a conventional shell, but communication demands the pre-existence of some conventions which are familiar to the person communicating and the person being communicated with, however rudimentary these may initially be. Whilst rejecting the restrictive conventions of what she called the 'materialist' novel, with its 'ill-fitting vestments of "two and thirty chapters",' she still felt that writing had to be formal – that the oyster needed *some* shell:

> I suppose the danger is the damned egotistical self; which ruins Joyce and Richardson to my mind: is one pliant and rich enough to provide a wall for the book from oneself without its becoming, as in Joyce and Richardson, narrowing and restricting?
>
> (*AWD* p. 23)

20

Once again we see a close affinity between Virginia Woolf's concern with the human and the literary problems of communication. Both the human individual and the novel need shells, walls, to define their distinctness as well as to provide a convention that allows communication to take place without what R. D. Laing calls 'loss of self' – or its literary equivalent. But walls can quickly become restrictive and instead of facilitating communication can prevent it.

Virginia Woolf was certainly aware of this danger as much in human as in literary terms. The year after *Mrs. Dalloway* was first published, the following ruminative passage appeared in her diary:

> Two resolute, sunburnt, dusty girls in jerseys and short skirts, with packs on their backs, city clerks, or secretaries, tramping along the road in the hot sunshine at Ripe. My instinct at once throws up a screen, which condemns them: I think them in every way angular, awkward and self-assertive. But all this is a great mistake. These screens shut me out. Have no screens, for screens are made out of our own integument; and get at the thing itself, which has nothing whatever in common with a screen. The screen-making habit, though, is so universal that probably it preserves our sanity. If we had not this device for shutting people off from our sympathies we might perhaps dissolve utterly; separateness would be impossible. But the screens are in the excess; not the sympathy.

$$(AWD \text{ p. } 97)$$

This passage seems to me to be extraordinarily rich and suggestive. Screens, walls, shells are necessary, or identity – whether human or literary – dissolves utterly. But although it is impossible to do without screens, they are 'in the excess' she feels, and it is more important to break them down than to build them up. Once again I think that we see a genuine desire to achieve that human communion that Virginia Woolf feels is lacking in her society. It is perhaps appropriate at this point to ask why it was the screens, rather than the sympathy, that were in the excess.

Alienation is a word that has a wide currency today, and is often used to mean little more than a vague feeling of not

21

being thoroughly at home in whatever situation the sufferer may find himself. My own use of the term is more specific, and is used to describe a set of phenomena which are brought into being by a very well-defined set of social circumstances. This use of the word, which is apparently too recent to be included in even the Addenda of the Shorter Oxford English Dictionary, is one which is taken from Marx's use of such words as *entäussern* and *entfremden* in his writing – particularly the early writing. Modern apologists for our social system have often tended to ignore the central aspect of Marx's use of this term in their own application of it in various contexts. Many writers on 'industrial relations', for example, speak of the need to prevent the worker from becoming alienated from his work, without mentioning that what Marx saw as the fundamental cause of alienation was the existence of private property. The worker puts something of himself into the product he creates, and yet this product belongs to someone else, and so he is alienated from a part of his own being, and from other people. As Marx says, the worker thus becomes poorer the more he produces, and consequently he is not only estranged from himself, but from what Marx calls his *species*, because he is forced to consider himself as an isolated individual in competition with others, rather than as a 'universal', as Marx expresses it. The basic contradiction in capitalist society, runs the argument, is that men must co-operate in the *production* of wealth to survive, which ensures that men do have something basic in common as they collectively transform external nature, but so far as the *ownership* of wealth is concerned, men are in competition with one another, are alienated from other men.

Now there are few members of the industrial proletariat in *Mrs. Dalloway,* but this does not mean to say that characters in the novel are unaffected by the situation I have described. As Marx says:

> . . . everything which appears in the worker as an *activity of alienation, of estrangement*, appears in the non-worker as a *state of alienation, of estrangement*.

> (*EPM* p. 119)

The reason why Clarissa *appears* to be a different person to different people is that she lives in a society in which it is essen-

22

tial for the successful individual to *be* a different person in different circumstances and with different people. As a result, Clarissa can never satisfactorily answer the worrying question, 'Who am I?'. It is instructive to compare Clarissa with Dickens's character Wemmick, in *Great Expectations*. Wemmick is, simply, two different people depending upon whether he is at work or at leisure. To quote Marx again:

> The worker therefore only feels himself outside his work, and in his work feels outside himself. He is at home when he is not working, and when he is working he is not at home.
>
> (*EPM* p. 110)

When Pip, in *Great Expectations*, asks Wemmick a question in the latter's home, he gets a different answer from that given when he asks the same question at work. Significantly, if we think of *Mrs. Dalloway*, Wemmick's work is in London, and his home is, literally, his castle. The drawbridge at his home symbolises adequately those defences – walls, screens or shell – with which he has to surround his humanity. He has a self suitable for the cash-nexus society of work, and a self suitable for the repressed *species* sense which can emerge at home. Brecht, in *The Good Woman of Setzuan*, makes much the same point. After his heroine has been visited by the Gods and given the money to start a business, she finds that she can continue to be 'good', or she can become a successful businesswoman, but she cannot do both as they involve totally contradictory sets of attitudes towards other people. This irreconcilability of private goodness and public success is not native to the human condition, Brecht suggests, but to a society founded on the sort of contradiction that I have mentioned.

Ralph Denham, a character in Virginia Woolf's *Night and Day*, feels that at the age of twenty-nine he can pride himself upon a life:

> ... rigidly divided into the hours of work and those of dreams; the two lived side by side without harming each other.
>
> (*NAD* p. 130)

Later on in the novel, however, the two *do* start to harm each other just as they do, briefly, for Wemmick.

*Mrs. Dalloway* is saturated with the problems of a society

which embodies – and in that sense causes – alienation. Not only are the characters in the novel alienated from one another, but the book itself is an attempt to overcome artistically the novelist's alienation from her reading public. The 'oyster' of *Mrs. Dalloway* needs a shell in which to secrete itself much as characters in the novel do – both as a way of protecting an essential identity and also as a means of communication. What is more, *Mrs. Dalloway* needs a very new sort of novelistic shell. The more the important life experienced by men and women in a particular society is a public one, then the more the novelist or artist can communicate this central importance through public, observable characteristics. The more that the important life experienced by men and women in a particular society is at least partially private, however, then the more the novelist is obliged to *create* public conventions to convey that for which none exist outside art.

The words 'to whom?' recur a number of times in *Mrs. Dalloway*, (and in *The Waves*), and are associated with most of the major characters in the novel – Rezia (p. 27), Peter Walsh (p. 65), Septimus (p. 75) and Clarissa herself (p. 135). All of these characters feel that they have something to do, give or say – but to whom they do not know. It seems possible that Virginia Woolf's offering – her novel – is made with as little confidence about the identity of the recipient. Ann Banfield, in an article entitled 'Narrative Style and the Grammar of Direct and Indirect Speech',[6] has argued that there is a literary style in English with no speaker or narrator, in which the characteristics of Direct and Indirect speech are mixed in such a way as to combine many of the characteristics of both speech forms. She cites *Mrs. Dalloway* as an example of a novel filled with this 'free indirect style' as she calls it, and in the course of a detailed analysis of the first nine sentences of the novel she notes how the novel manages to combine the impression of a narrator talking to a reader and Clarissa Dalloway talking herself – but, we may ask, to whom? The truth is that the style allows the privacy of Clarissa's thoughts to be carried almost parasitically on the wings of the narrator-reader address. To this extent the very style of *Mrs. Dalloway* is totally appropriate to what is to be conveyed, as whilst actually communicating the inner 'oyster' of Clarissa and other characters to the reader it also conveys their lack of anyone with whom they can really communicate. Perhaps analysis of a specific passage will help to make this point more adequately. After having visited Clarissa, Peter Walsh returns to his hotel, where a letter from Clarissa awaits him – a curious discovery for him to make, as we have already learned that:

> . . . they might be parted for hundreds of years, she and Peter; she never wrote a letter and his were dry sticks . . .
>
> (*MD* p. 9)

Clarissa's behaviour here reminds us of Sue Bridehead in Hardy's *Jude the Obscure,* who frequently follows up an unsatisfactory personal encounter with Jude with a far more friendly and open written message.

After reading her letter, Peter Walsh is upset and the following passage occurs (one feels the need to use a neutral expression here; it might not be strictly accurate to say that the following thoughts go through his mind, as some may not have done):

> These hotels are not consoling places. Far from it. Any number of people had hung up their hats on those pegs. Even the flies, if you thought of it, had settled on other people's noses. As for the cleanliness which hit him in the face, it wasn't cleanliness, so much as bareness, frigidity; a thing that had to be. Some arid matron made her rounds at dawn sniffing, peering, causing blue-nosed maids to scour, for all the world as if the next visitor were a joint of meat to be served on a perfectly clean platter. For sleep, one bed; for sitting in, one arm-chair; for cleaning one's teeth and shaving one's chin, one tumbler, one looking-glass. Books, letters, dressing-gown, slipped about on the impersonality of the horse-hair like incongruous impertinences. And it was Clarissa's letter that made him see all this.
>
> (*MD* pp. 170, 171)

*alienating peter dehumanising him*

It's worth noting the clash of two discrete value-systems symbolised in the hotel and the letter here. It is the human contact with Clarissa through her letter that opens Peter Walsh's eyes to the impersonality of the hotel in which he is staying, in which he is treated more as an object (meat on a platter) than as a

81064

person. But let us consider the extent to which we can separate thoughts or statements made or thought by Peter Walsh, from those to be attributed to the narrator. The first four sentences of the passage appear to give us Peter Walsh's stream of consciousness, although the first sentence *could* be an authorial interjection, and there is a certain ambiguity about the origin of all four sentences. The fifth sentence must be spoken by a narrator, as Peter Walsh is referred to as 'him', yet nevertheless, it seems to incorporate the thought-patterns of Peter Walsh which have been introduced early on in the passage. When we get to the arid matron, we feel that we are being addressed by Peter Walsh again, but once more we cannot exclude the narrator from any authorial intervention here for sure. Perhaps the most striking example is the sentence, 'And it was Clarissa's letter that made him see all this.' This could be either an authorial interjection, explaining what has caused the line of thought that Peter Walsh had just developed, or it could refer to a realisation on Peter Walsh's own part that this is the explanation of the direction of his recent thoughts. There is no way of being sure one way or the other.

There are many similar passages in *Mrs. Dalloway*. Although the 'common reader' may not be directly aware of the sort of ambiguity that I have been discussing, he will almost certainly feel that there is something odd in the way that the thoughts of different characters are conveyed to him. I have said that the novelist cannot be a solipsist, but the novelist can convey the experience of isolation, however paradoxical this may appear. The reader has the feeling that he has become an invisible observer – not just of characters' external behaviour or even conscious thoughts, as in the classical novel – but of those thought processes of which characters themselves are only partially aware. Along with this goes the feeling that the direction of the novel is not an erratic or formless one but is associated with the organising presence of a narrative figure who knows and directs without disturbing the reality being conveyed. Thus Virginia Woolf avoids the common mistake of assuming that a work of art has to be what it is concerned with, whilst yet managing to make its subject of concern – human isolation – real for the reader. The whole novel raises the question 'to whom?' in the mind of the reader. From whence is our informa-

26

tion coming, for whom – if anyone – is it intended? This impression of knowledge without relationships, of an understanding of those aspects of human beings which are beyond human perception, represents an artistic triumphing over a human contradiction. In *Mrs. Dalloway*, miraculously, the oyster is revealed without breaking the shell.

# 3
# DIVIDED SELVES

'SEPTIMUS' ALIENATION

REASON FOR SEPTIMUS' ALIENATION

There seems little doubt that Virginia Woolf's experience of what she called 'madness' contributed to her sense of the dissolution of human identity. Yet it would be a mistake to see the whole question of self-dissolution or division in *Mrs. Dalloway* as a clinical matter. Certain social forces which had been developing in British society for some time were making a sharp division between the public and the private necessary for more and more people. It is worth remarking on the fact that in one sense Septimus Smith, the 'mad' character in *Mrs. Dalloway,* is *not* 'divided' in the way that other characters are, and it is arguable that it is his attempt to synthesise the public and the private that results in his inability to conform to the requirements of his society. Joan Bennett has suggested that after 1919 Virginia Woolf was not capable of including the clearly defined human character among those aspects of life in which she could believe with conviction.[7] Her experience of madness was probably a contributory factor in this change of attitude, but more important social developments – both on a wider scale and also relating to her particular social circle – are certainly involved. Her own artistic development has parallels in the development of other major contemporary writers and other artists. In 1923, in the early stages of writing *Mrs. Dalloway,* she stated in her diary that character '. . . is dissipated into shreds now . . .', and this theme recurs constantly in her writing at this time. In 'Mr. Bennett and Mrs. Brown', written in 1924, she 'hazarded the assertion' that '. . . in or about December, 1910, human character changed'. The date mentioned seems almost certainly to refer to the first post-Impressionist exhibition in London, which was organised by Roger Fry. It is worth linking her views on 'time', 'life' and 'reality' not only with Einstein's *Theory of Relativity,* but also the work of Joyce, Proust, Kafka and Musil.[8] Another name that might be added to this list is that of Joseph Conrad, of whom Virginia Woolf remarked that he was composed of two people who had nothing in common. In *Mr. Conrad: A Con-*

28

*versation,* she suggested that Conrad was not one and simple, but complex and many – words almost identical to those that Bernard, in *The Waves,* uses at one point to describe himself.

When we turn to *Mrs. Dalloway,* therefore, and consider the relationship between the divided selves of a single character, we need to bear in mind that we are dealing not with an eccentric offshoot of Virginia Woolf's madness, but with a specific example of a phenomenon which appears so insistently in the literature of this period that it suggests some common, fundamental reality underlying it. In her 1928 *Introduction* to the novel, Virginia Woolf claimed that a first version of the novel was written in which Septimus Smith did not appear, and that he was introduced later as Clarissa Dalloway's 'double'. It is as if the novelist has taken the divided selves of one character, and has turned them into two people. In this same *Introduction,* Virginia Woolf also informed the reader that in this first version of the novel, Clarissa was, '. . . originally to kill herself, or perhaps merely to die at the end of the party'. Kitty Maxse, who, according to Quentin Bell's biography of Virginia Woolf, was to some extent the model for the character of Clarissa Dalloway, died suddenly in 1922 after a fall from the top of a flight of stairs. Virginia Woolf believed that she had committed suicide and this may be one possible explanation of the rather opaque suggestions in Virginia Woolf's notes to the novel that Clarissa's progress from one level to another up her stairs has some sort of symbolic significance – a significance which the completed novel does not manage to convey in any clear form.

We do not need the evidence of her *Introduction* to see that there are close affinities and relationships between Septimus and Clarissa, even though they never meet. Virginia Woolf's fear that the reviewers would say that the mad scenes did not connect with the Dalloway scenes seems to have been unwarranted. Poetic techniques are used to relate Septimus and Clarissa with each other in the novel; both are beak-nosed, bird-like, associated with similar patterns of imagery and literary echoes such as the refrain from *Cymbeline* (which is sung in the play to Imogen, in the mistaken belief that she is dead). Septimus thinks that 'something tremendous [is] about to happen', Clarissa that 'something awful was about to happen'. Such parallels and contrasts can be added to. Clarissa 'feels' the death of Septimus whereas he had been unable to feel the death of Evans (it is not correct to say, as does Leon Edel, that it is a common 'failure to feel' that makes Septimus and Clarissa doubles).[9]

What do these parallels and contrasts add up to? Winifred Holtby sees the relationship between the two characters as metaphysical and psychological,[10] which may be the case but which certainly needs further elucidation. Perhaps more germane to our enquiry at this point is the insistence upon the *social* significance of the relationship of the two characters that Bernard Blackstone makes:

> Without the Galloways there would be no Warren Smiths. Behind the Galloways there rises the massive edifice of civilisation, the Houses of Parliament, St. Paul's Cathedral, the War Office, the Law Courts, the professional classes, Harley Street.[11]

'Civilisation' is a trigger-word in *Mrs. Dalloway,* used ironically rather than in a laudatory sense, and whatever one may think about the restrictiveness of Virginia Woolf's social and political vision there are some significant flashes of insight into the relationships between personal and social phenomena in the novel. Is Sally Seton's suggestion that the well-bred but secretly lustful Hugh Whitbread is 'responsible' for the fate of 'those poor girls in Piccadilly' so far-fetched? Certainly Richard Dalloway – who has an unusually well-developed sense of social relationships for a Conservative Member of Parliament – sees prostitution to be the fault of our social system, and Peter Walsh even feels that:

> . . . God knows, the rascals who get hanged for battering the brains of a girl out in a train do less harm on the whole than Hugh Whitbread and his kindness !
>
> (*MD* p. 190)

Now *Mrs. Dalloway* is not *Waiting for Lefty,* and it would be absurd to interpret it as a developed Marxist analysis of Virginia Woolf's society. But on the other hand it would, I feel, be equally misleading to ignore the fact that it consistently tries to uncover hidden relationships both between different characters, and also between characters and social institutions. In many cases a character – Sir William Bradshaw for example – represents an aspect of her society rather than a particular example of human individuality for Virginia Woolf. I think that the few fleeting references to prostitution in *Mrs. Dalloway* show how Virginia Woolf was concerned to relate individual and social phenomena. Put simply, I think that it is *true* that there is a connection between the hypocritical attitudes of Hugh Whitbread with his external correctness and concealed lust and the 'poor girls in Piccadilly'. It is probable that very little that Marx wrote would have interested Virginia Woolf directly, but the following comment might perhaps have caught her attention:

> Prostitution is only a *specific* expression of the *general* prostitution of the *labourer,* and since it is a relationship in which falls not the prostitute alone, but also the one who prostitutes – and the latter's abomination is still greater – the capitalist, etc., also comes under this head.
>
> *(EPM* p. 133(n))

It is certainly important to be constantly aware that Septimus is a victim of the war, whilst the Dalloways are representative of politics and government. Years before the writing of *Three Guineas* Virginia Woolf had a very clear idea of the connection between the brutality of war and the 'screen-making habits' of English males of the governing classes. I want it to be clear that I am not arguing for an interpretation of *Mrs. Dalloway* in terms of an overt, consistent political message. What I am saying is that Virginia Woolf saw important connections between social institutions and individual characteristics, and that the relationship between Clarissa and Septimus in the novel is not just metaphysical and psychological, but has an important *social* dimension too.

I would suggest, therefore, that Septimus's madness plays a complex and multiple role in the novel. On one level it is an extreme *symbol* of that alienation from human contact that all of the characters suffer from to a greater or a lesser extent. On another level, as a result of the specifically social links which are drawn between Septimus (who lost the ability to feel through the war), and characters such as Sir William

31

Bradshaw (who is a servant and eager supporter of that 'civili-sation' which is associated with the war), Septimus's madness is seen as the *result* of particular pressures engendered by an alienating society.

Certainly, the introduction of a mad character into the novel allows the presentation of an extreme form of alienation. Mad-ness is the supreme isolator, and the more a man needs other men, the more madness is feared. Samuel Johnson, that most fervent believer in man's social nature and the most suspicious critic of enthusiasm and private experiences of truth, in the midst of experiencing a stroke which was partially to paralyse him, prayed to God that however He might afflict his body, He should spare his mind. Madness cuts off Septimus from nearly all real human contact:

> But Rezia could not understand him. Dr. Holmes was such a kind man. He was so interested in Septimus. He only wanted to help them, he said. He had four little children and he had asked her to tea, she told Septimus.
>
> So he was deserted.
>
> (*MD* p. 102)

Dr Holmes's invitation to his wife makes Septimus feel deserted in just the same way that Lady Bruton's invitation to her husband makes Clarissa feel that she is alone. Both need people and are terrified of solitude, but Clarissa, although often ap-parently teetering on the edge of the horror that encompasses Septimus, has certain lifelines which preserve her. Both Septimus and Clarissa make gifts. But Septimus's gift of his life only completes his isolation in death, symbolised by the enclos-ing ambulance representative, as Peter Walsh feels, of 'civilisa-tion'. Clarissa's gift of her party, on the other hand, really does succeed in bringing people together for a short time.

> Communication is health; communication is happiness. Communication, he muttered.
>
> 'What are you saying, Septimus?' Rezia asked, wild with terror, for he was talking to himself.
>
> (*MD* pp. 103, 104)

The bitter irony of this 'exchange' contrasts with the fact that even though Richard cannot bring himself to tell Clarissa that he loves her, there is still enough contact between the two to preserve Clarissa's sanity. Thus when she hears of Septimus's death, Clarissa understands that

Death was defiance. Death was an attempt to communicate, people feeling the impossibility of reaching the centre which, mystically, evaded them; closeness drew apart; rapture faded; one was alone. There was an embrace in death.

(*MD* p. 202)

*was a reverse from alienation*

This passage echoes many of the phrases in an earlier passage describing Clarissa's vicarious indulgence in the described sexual passion of another woman

Then, for that moment, she had seen an illumination; a match burning in a crocus; an innermeaning almost expressed. But the close withdrew; the hard softened.

(*MD* p. 36)

The embrace that Septimus finds in death is sought because he cannot find it in that human contact achieved momentarily at her party that recharges Clarissa's spiritual reserves. The traditional association of sex and death surely stems from a recognition that sex involves some extinction of privacy, some breaking down of the walls of the self, that prefigures the complete extinction of the self in death.

Septimus's dying words – 'I'll give it you!' – are thus extremely significant, as they point to the thing that both he and Clarissa most want to do – to *give*. The final extinction of self that Septimus throws himself to in his suicide jump is described in terms that have been used to describe heterosexual passion earlier on, because Virginia Woolf sees close and significant parallels between the act of giving a life and giving in sex. It is Clarissa's fear of 'losing herself' as Septimus loses himself that accounts for her lack of 'something central that permeated', for her inability to give herself – as we say, 'body and soul' – to a sexual relationship. It is thus revealing that there is a distinctly sexual element in Clarissa's imagination of Septimus's death-scene:

He had thrown himself from a window. Up had flashed the ground; through him, blundering, bruising, went the rusty

33

spikes. There he lay with a thud, thud, thud in his brain, and then a suffocation of blackness.

(*MD* p. 202)

Clarissa concludes that there is an embrace in death, but in the descriptions of her inability to give herself to either Peter Walsh or, sexually, to Richard, we can see her fear that there is death in an embrace, that abandonment to passion is beyond her because she fears the loss of self – seen symbolically magnified in Septimus's death – that it threatens.

I have said that in *Mrs. Dalloway* madness is seen both as a symbol and a result of alienation. Because madness does cut the individual off from other people, it is to be expected that many of the characteristics resulting from mental disorder may resemble those which result from a society which denies its members full human contact. Furthermore, such a society would be likely to exacerbate any predisposition towards mental disorder in an individual who had difficulty in making contact with other people. Even if Septimus were a real person and not a character in a novel, it would be difficult to say whether or not the need to shut out the horrors of war caused, or encouraged, his inability to feel. What one can say is that once such an inability has become apparent, a society in which it is necessary not to feel for other people in certain circumstances will not encourage recovery.

Septimus is possessed of many of the paradoxical impulses that recent research has revealed to be common in cases of schizophrenia, and in which we can sometimes see, albeit in a distorted or magnified form, impulses that are experienced by those not suffering from any mental disorder. Septimus wishes to communicate but is scared of self-exposure, and his 'madness' clearly has a defensive function for him, which the following passage, with its vague echoes of *King Lear,* points to:

But he would not go mad. He would shut his eyes; he would see no more.

(*MD* p. 26)

In this instance, Septimus's eye-lids are screens which preserve his sense of identity, which prevent him from 'dissolving utterly'. But screens, we remember, can threaten to destroy that which

34

they protect, just as it is possible that in shutting herself off from Peter Walsh, Clarissa may have caused the death of her soul. When Septimus shuts his eyes in sleep, much later in the novel, the destructive side of this attempt to preserve his self becomes apparent:

He was very tired. He was very happy. He would sleep. He shut his eyes. But directly he saw nothing the sounds of the game became fainter and stranger and sounded like the cries of people seeking and not finding, and passing farther and farther away. They had lost him!

He started up in terror. What did he see? The plate of bananas on the sideboard. Nobody was there (Rezia had taken the child to its mother; it was bedtime). That was it: to be alone for ever. That was the doom pronounced in Milan . . .

(*MD* pp. 159, 160) 'screen'

It was in Milan that he realised the implications of his inability to feel the death of Evans. An inability to feel may have temporary advantages, but it impoverishes and isolates, it eventually destroys what it is intended to protect. As Marx expresses it, man's relation to himself only becomes objective and actual through his relation to the other man, and Septimus's inability to feel the death of the 'other man' leads to a loss of what R. D. Laing calls ontological security.

In an unpublished comment written at the time she was working on *Mrs. Dalloway*, Virginia Woolf suggested that Septimus was to be:

. . . only real in so far as [Rezia] sees him. Otherwise to exist in his view of things: which is always to be contrasting with Mrs. Dalloways. (*sic*)[12]

Septimus, in other words, has a very low level of ontological security. We all exist and are real only in so far as other people see us, but we do not normally need to be seen by other people all the time. Septimus lacks the reserves of strength given by a secure sense of self, and needs constant, immediate self-confirmation through contact with Rezia. Once again we can note that this is an exaggerated version of a normal human need, rather than something totally removed from any familiar

35

human experience. Septimus lacks a secure sense of self and therefore needs another person more than is usual; Miss Kilman, who describes herself, interestingly, as a wheel without a tyre at one point in the novel, lacks a close personal relationship, and thus needs to develop a more than normally secure sense of self – much is made in the novel of her 'armour'.

Virginia Woolf talks of screens; we can perhaps raid the vocabulary of the astronaut to suggest that the 'normal' person has various forms of emotional air-lock which allows in only that which does not threaten the individual's ontological security, and which enable him to communicate with other people. Septimus has no such air-lock apart from Rezia, and so the attempt to separate him from her is a threat to his very existence as an independent human being. Another comment of Virginia Woolf's on Septimus is interesting in this context:

> [Septimus] might be left vague – as a mad person is – not so much character as an idea – This is what is painful to her [Rezia] – becomes generalised – universalised. So can be partly R; partly me.[13]

If we wish to know what this generalisation and universalisation consist of, we need to have some way of relating Septimus's isolation to the situation of other characters in the novel – particularly Clarissa – who are not 'mad' in the same sense.

Leonard Woolf has claimed that there was a real distinction between Virginia Woolf's mad and sane states, which could be expressed as the distinction between an 'awareness and acceptance of the outside world and a rational reaction to it' and 'a refusal to admit or accept facts in the outside world'. The distiction is one that can fruitfully be applied to the distinction between Septimus and Clarissa, and yet in spite of this there are important parallels as well as contrasts between their respective situations. Septimus's internal alienation is compounded by the fact that his only contact with a human reality is through one who is herself an alien;[14] Rezia feels that, 'I am alone; I am alone!'. Clarissa too feels isolated from other people although she desperately needs them, and it is worth asking whether her rejection of Peter Walsh is to be seen as in some way parallel to Septimus's inability to feel the death of Evans. R. D. Laing has written that we all share the psychotic's paradoxical need to reveal and conceal himself, and that in most cases we have reached the more or less satisfactory solution of having our secrets and our needs to confess. He suggests that it is when we tell our first lie that we realise that in certain respects we are irredeemably alone, and that 'within the territory of ourselves there can be only our footprints'. This phrase is strikingly similar to one to be found in Virginia Woolf's essay 'On Being Ill' (a situation in which the individual feels more than normally cut off from other people): 'There is a virgin forest in each; a snowfield where even the print of birds' feet is unknown.' Laing claims that genuine privacy is the basis of genuine relationship, and it is perhaps to preserve the last few square feet of untrodden snow in his soul that Septimus kills himself.

My insistence on the importance of human privacy may seem to run counter to the general drift of my argument that the disjunction between the public and the private is a product of human alienation, and is to be regretted. I think that it is important to make a distinction between a situation where the private and public selves of an individual are not only completely separate but are contradictory, which I associate with alienation, and a situation where the individual enjoys some 'untrodden snow in his soul' which confirms his own human individuality without implicitly or explicitly denying the human individuality of others. Having said this, it is necessary to add that in a society not founded upon the sort of contradictions to which I have drawn attention, the individual would (and does) feel far less need for a secure area of personal privacy either within him or herself, or within an exclusive personal relationship. Whether such a need could ever disappear completely in a different social situation, I am not sure.

Septimus is irredeemably alone because, unlike Clarissa, he has completely shut himself off from feeling rather than taking risks and exposing his vulnerability – although to this it must be added that his experience of the war placed a greater pressure on him than did Clarissa's more restricted social experience. Clarissa's parties, as I want to argue more fully in a later chapter, involve vulnerability and risk as well as being an offering; they enable her to regenerate her sense of identity through the development of relationships based on openness and honesty. Earlier I drew a parallel between Virginia Woolf's description of the creative process of writing a novel, and Clarissa's behaviour at her party. In both cases some alternation between retreat and exposure, privacy and communion is necessary. Septimus has lost this ability, and is fixed in a privacy inescapable until he makes that tragic contact with Rezia immediately before his death. Septimus's form of madness is simply loneliness intensified beyond the point of human endurance.[15] Clarissa may shut herself off from a concern with the persecuted Armenians (or Albanians), but her ability to feel Septimus's death, while it makes her vulnerable, keeps her sane.

Some screens are necessary. Whereas Septimus thinks about large questions of life and death but feels nothing on a more immediately personal level, Clarissa:

> . . . cared much more for her roses than for the Armenians. Hunted out of existence, maimed, frozen, the victims of cruelty and injustice (she had heard Richard say so over and over again) – no, she could feel nothing for the Albanians, or was it the Armenians? but she loved her roses (didn't that help the Armenians?) – the only flowers she could bear to see cut.
>
> (*MD* p. 133)

The implication is, as T. S. Eliot puts it in 'Burnt Norton', that human kind cannot bear very much reality. The impossibility of reconciling a knowledge of the movements of large social and political forces with the values of one's personal life stems, surely, from the fact that public and private lives are based on different and mutually exclusive value systems. Clarissa's choice of her roses rather than the Armenians can be contrasted with the choice made by Doris Kilman, who:

> . . . would do anything for the Russians, starved herself for the Austrians, but in private inflicted positive torture, so insensitive was she, dressed in a green mackintosh coat.
>
> (*MD* p. 14)

It is difficult to avoid the feeling that a false pair of alternatives is being presented to the reader here, although there is the example of Richard Dalloway's concern for Armenians *and* roses that needs to be considered.

38

Why should Virginia Woolf apparently load the dice at this point? I would like to suggest that in a deeper sense it is true that, given her belief in the unchangeable nature of her world, Clarissa cannot reconcile a love for humanity at large with a love for those symbolic roses. Boris Kuznetsov, writing about Dostoyevsky, has shown how eagerly writers in the nineteenth century seized on the example of an Euclidean harmony which ignored microscopic processes as a parallel to the harmony of their social order which also ignored microscopic processes – that is, the fates of individual men and women. He argues that just as the physicist is still trying to find an order which encompasses both the macro- and microscopic process, so too:

> Modern notions of moral harmony require that an individual existence be determined by its importance to the collective destiny.[16]

This is the sort of reconciliation that neither Septimus, nor Miss Kilman, nor Clarissa – any more than Wemmick or Brecht's heroine – can achieve, for all of them accept a social order which contains a fundamental disjunction between public and private, individual and collective destiny.

Miss Kilman, as much as Charles Tansley in *To the Lighthouse* and *The Man who loved his Kind* in Virginia Woolf's short story of that name, would like to have personal relationships based on love rather than aggression and competition, and we are told at the beginning of *Mrs. Dalloway* that Clarissa would like to have been 'interested in politics like a man', but this sort of reconciliation is open to neither of them. The one character who succeeds in reconciling public and private is Septimus – and the success drives him mad.

I am perhaps giving Virginia Woolf the benefit of a little too much special pleading at this point, however. There is no doubt that Clarissa Dalloway's attitudes reflect a partly culpable blindness on the part of Virginia Woolf to the fate of those not immediately before her. Quentin Bell tells a revealing anecdote about how the realities of unemployment were brought home to her only when a fainting unemployed girl knocked at her door and asked for a drink of water. Whatever the contradictions in our society, they do not force this sort of blindness upon its members.

Virginia Woolf was deeply suspicious of those with causes, in which she detected egotism and the desire to force other people's souls. In her diary in 1923 she wrote that she was 'a great deal interested suddenly in my book. I want to bring in the despicableness of people like Ott.' 'Ott' was Lady Ottoline Morrell. In *Beginning Again*, Leonard Woolf commented that:

> [The Morrells] were leading members of that stage army of British progressives who can be relied upon to sign a letter to *The Times* supporting an unpopular cause or protesting against a pogrom or judicial murder.

> (*BA* p. 198)

The suggestion is that anyone who pretends to feel deeply about 'a pogrom or judicial murder' must be being hypocritical. Now it may well be true that there was more than a residual element of posturing in the causes adopted as their own by the Morrells, but many readers will surely feel that if so, such posturing is to be preferred to an inability to feel anything for the Albanians or the Armenians.

Lady Bruton, who writes a letter to *The Times* with the aid of Hugh Whitbread and Richard Dalloway, is not given the benefit of supporting such unimpeachable causes however, and is seen to be obsessed by what appears to be near forcible emigration (doubtless the more comfortable contemporary term, 'repatriation', would have appealed to her). She wants to push people around against their wills just as Sir William Bradshaw wants to move Septimus against his will, and both have the symbolic backing of the state. Whilst rejecting the view that roses are more important than Armenians (and there is no definite authorial support for this attitude of Clarissa's – or criticism of it), we need to remember that causes, political and religious, can sometimes make their adherents forget the humanity of those for whom they are ostensibly striving. We also need to remember that a separation of private from public morality is fundamental to capitalist society.

I think that there are interesting parallels that can be drawn between *Mrs. Dalloway* and Joseph Conrad's *The Secret Agent* in this context. Obviously, on one level, the latter novel suggests that people who espouse causes end by treating other people as tokens to be manipulated rather than as people, but there is a more significant parallel than that. In *The Secret Agent* we again have a mentally-disturbed or retarded character – Stevie – who is unable to reach a satisfactory relationship with the world which includes sympathy but excludes horror. Horrified by the condition of a cab-horse, Stevie is even more horrified to learn from the cabman that the security of the latter's family *depends* on the horse's ill-treatment:

> 'Poor! Poor!' stammered out Stevie, pushing his hands deeper into his pockets with convulsive sympathy. He could say nothing; for his tenderness to all pain and all misery, the desire to make the horse happy and the cabman happy, had reached the point of a bizarre longing to take them to bed with him. And that, he knew, was impossible. For Stevie was not mad. It was, as it were, a symbolic longing . . .

In a society where not only does the happiness of cabmen seem to depend on the unhappiness of cab-horses, but where the happiness of one man can depend upon the unhappiness of another man, then such symbolic longings will, in default of a desire to change society itself, tend to emerge.

Other interesting parallels between the two novels are worthy of note. There is a strong suggestion in *Mrs. Dalloway* that Septimus's insanity is in some ways a logical – even sane – response to the insanity of war, a paradox explored with remorseless logic by Joseph Heller in *Catch 22.* Certainly it is only by inhumanity – that is, obliviousness to the pains of the Armenians – that Clarissa retains her humanity and avoids madness, just as Mr Verloc in *The Secret Agent,* who thinks of himself as just doing a job of work and remains oblivious to the fact that it results in people's deaths, stays sane. Significantly *The Secret Agent,* like *Mrs. Dalloway,* is set in London, and it is worthy of note that Mr Verloc's 'front' (revealing word) for his nefarious activities is the sale of pornography – the ultimate symbol of the reduction of human beings to objects alienated from one another. Most of all, Conrad, like Virginia Woolf in her portrayal of Septimus, brings out the *self-destructiveness* of the isolation which these conditions produce: the ghastly figure of the professor, living in his own fantasy world and prepared to blow himself up with the explosive he carries continually if the police attempt to arrest him, is a symbol of something that goes far beyond *The Secret Agent* in its significance.

Returning to England after the war, Septimus feels, as his train leaves Newhaven, that it might be possible that the world itself is without meaning. The contrast between his experiences during the war and the 'civilisation' which was responsible for the war but which appears to be unaware of it is too much for Septimus, too great to have any meaning imposed upon it. Whatever impression of social rarification the reader of *Mrs. Dalloway* may initially receive, the novel constantly uncovers connections between many seemingly diverse phenomena. The first reference in the novel to a suppression of the emotions in order to preserve 'public' decorum comes on the second page, when Lady Bexborough opens a bazaar with the telegram announcing the death of her favourite son in her hand. The war is thus related to that 'manliness' that conceals natural emotions and drives a wedge between the public and the private. Clarissa thanks Heaven that the war is over, but it is not over for the shell-shocked Septimus who relives it in his memory, and shows in a heightened way what Virginia Woolf shows in many other characters, that we 'are', in part, what we have been. *Mrs. Dalloway* is saturated with references to the war, which remains a lingering symbolic presence throughout the novel, and is specifically associated, through Holmes and Bradshaw, with the state and with the habit of separating public and private experience. Septimus cannot reconcile post-war Newhaven with his war-time experiences; he lacks that 'sense of proportion' that allows Bradshaw to ignore awkward connections, relationships. Rezia cannot understand Septimus's obsessions, for '. . . such things happen to every one. Every one has friends who were killed in the war. Every one gives up something when they marry.'

In view of the symbolic significance that the war comes to have in the novel, we are not surprised to learn that Lady Bruton 'could have led troops to attack', and that although Doris Kilman lost her post for attacking jingoism in the war, she has become possessed of 'the power and taciturnity of some prehistoric monster armoured for primeval warfare'. Septimus claims to have stopped feeling in the war, but we have Rezia's recollection that he was 'only suffering sometimes through this

42

terrible war', and at his death he is saluted in the manner of men killed in battle by the apron of Mrs Filmer, which resembles a flag:

> 'The War?' the patient asked. The European War – that little shindy of schoolboys with gunpowder? Had he served with distinction? He really forgot. In the War itself he had failed.
> 'Yes, he served with the greatest distinction,' Rezia assured the doctor; 'he was promoted.'
>
> (*MD* p. 106)

The paradox is presented forcibly here; Septimus feels that his outward distinction in the war is really a failure. The word 'failure' gathers around itself a number of pregnant echoes in *Mrs. Dalloway*, and becomes suggestive of its opposite. To fail in a system that is inhuman may be testimony to one's humanity, and it is to the credit of characters such as Septimus and Peter Walsh (who is referred to as a failure on a number of occasions) that they do fail to measure up to the public standards of their society. Septimus's 'failure-in-success' is not confined to his war record:

> 'And they have the very highest opinion of you at your office?' Sir William murmured . . .
>
> (*MD* p. 106)

– just as they have of Wemmick.

It is Sir William's achievement of a sense of proportion which, in one of the most powerful passages in the novel, is revealed as life-denying and the real failure. The connection between Sir William's personal obnoxiousness and the state he defends and represents is made quite unambiguous.

> In short, this living or not living is an affair of our own? But there they were mistaken. Sir William had a friend in Surrey where they taught, what Sir William frankly admitted was a difficult art – a sense of proportion. There were, moreover, family affection; honour; courage; and a brilliant career. All of these had in Sir William a resolute champion. If they failed, he had to support him police and the good of society, which, he remarked very quietly, would take care,

down in Surrey, that these unsocial impulses, bred more than
anything by the lack of good blood, were held in control.

(*MD* pp. 112, 113)

Sir William's 'sense of proportion' involves a refusal to see that
the human values he appeals to are not to be reconciled with
the values of the state whose servant he is and whose authority
he upholds. His sense of proportion is an acceptance of hypo-
crisy, of the necessary disjunction of private and public values,
coupled with a brutal attack on those who seek to reveal this
disjunction and to overcome it. Whereas Sir William's sense of
proportion is an acceptance of the inevitability of the self being
divided, what makes Septimus a sort of hero *manqué* is his
refusal to accept this division, and his willingness to accept
death in order to preserve his own existential unity.

# 4

# LOVE

'Love,' John Bayley has remarked, 'brings to a head this problem of identity.' For many of the characters in *Mrs. Dalloway* love, in different forms, appears both as a threat and as salvation; like so many other things in the novel its nature is seen to be two-edged and complex. Bayley also says that love may unite us or keep us apart, 'but it always reveals the differences between us'.[17] To love someone is to recognise their distinctness, their separateness from us, but the act of loving can, paradoxically, bring the loved one closer, can start to reduce this separateness. In *The Portrait of a Lady* Henry James observes that, 'The chief impression produced on Isabel's spirit by [Ralph Touchett's] criticism was that the passion of love separated its victim terribly from the loved object'. Unable to excuse her husband's behaviour to others except by claiming that he has been working too hard, Rezia concludes that, 'To love makes one solitary . . .'. Thinking of her youthful love for Sally Seton, Clarissa feels that '. . . nothing is so strange when one is in love . . . as the complete indifference of other people'. This separation can be a blessing or a curse. When Clarissa rejects Peter Walsh, we get the impression that she feels that marriage to him would cut her off from enriching relationships with other people – just as it does at Bourton. But in their brief reconciliation and contact before the final tragedy, Septimus and Rezia achieve a more fruitful sort of mutual privacy, where it is as if the walls of the self have expanded to include two:

> How it rejoiced her, that! Not for weeks had they laughed like this together, poking fun privately like married people. What she meant was that if Mrs. Filmer had come in, or Mrs. Peters or anybody, they would not have understood what she and Septimus were laughing at.
>
> *(MD* p. 157)

It is significant that immediately after this passage, Rezia pins a rose to the hat they are jointly making, a symbol that, throughout *Mrs. Dalloway*, represents those epiphanies in life in which human beings achieve some sort of enriching but secure communion.

Clarissa, we know, needs other people, and the plural is of crucial importance. After seeing Elizabeth and Miss Kilman out of the house, Clarissa recoils in horror from what she sees in their relationship:

> Love and religion! thought Clarissa, going back into the drawing-room, tingling all over. How detestable, how detestable they are!
>
> (*MD* p. 139)

In like manner, her immediate reaction to Peter's declaration that he is in love with the Indian Army Major's wife is that of mingled surprise and disgust: 'That he at his age should be sucked under in his little bow-tie by that monster!' The image brings to mind Septimus's graphic description of the attempted 'conversion' by Holmes and Bradshaw: 'The brute with the red nostrils was sniffing into every secret place!'

Love then can be a double-edged experience for characters in *Mrs. Dalloway*. It can provide a means of confirming one's own identity by seeing it admired by another, and it can take one out of oneself into an appreciation of the distinctness of another person. This positive aspect of love is a process rather than an event, a process which changes those who are in love, their relationships with each other, and with other people. But love has its negative side, where it resembles religion and conversion, where it involves a desire to subdue or consume the other person's identity. Thus the novel presents no simple attitude towards love, but a complex understanding that it must be evaluated in concrete terms taking into account both its larger context and its development. In *Night and Day* Katharine Hilbery finds that when she considers the interpretation of the word 'love' 'in each case it seemed to stand for something different, and yet for something unmistakable and not to be passed by'. Likewise in *Mrs. Dalloway* there is a need to recognise that love is 'something unmistakable and not to be passed by', but that its nature is not to be too easily simplified or generalised about.

Thus it is his *absence* of love that makes Sir William Bradshaw such a horrifying person, and in spite of her immediate reaction to Peter Walsh's admission that he is in love, Clarissa feels the need to move to a more positive qualification:

> And there's no flesh on his neck; his hands are red; and he's six months older than I am! her eye flashed back to her; but in her heart she felt, all the same; he is in love. He has that, she felt; he is in love.

> (*MD* p. 50)

I think that the ambiguity of Clarissa's attitude reflects the sort of paradox that I have suggested love involves, with its combination of a recognition of the *separateness* of another person, and a desire to break down this separateness to achieve a closer relationship or union. Like the novelist, the human individual must move between privacy and communion, between being 'together and apart'.

For this reason I feel that many critical attempts to 'fix' Virginia Woolf's attitude to love in the novel have been doomed to failure. One critic, for example, has seen a 'polarity of love and conversion' in the novel, which presents Clarissa with the necessity of making a moral choice between the two by which she creates her self:

> In the novel, love implies an attitude of allowance; letting others be; recognizing in them an inviolable private self. A character who experiences love has a sense of wonder at life, for he sees that it offers him the possibilities of both solitude and society. He is free to be himself, and yet he can come together with others in a close but unstultifying relationship.[18]

The suggestion that love offers the possibility of both solitude and society is well said, for in the scene immediately before Septimus's death we see that he and Rezia achieve a state of mutual contact which is nevertheless private. But it must be remembered that Clarissa is aware of the fact that Peter Walsh's love allows her anything but 'solitude and society'. Love can unite, but it can also consume, and this more sinister aspect of love is perhaps suggested by the metaphor of the spider's thread which is associated with Clarissa throughout the novel. The female spider, we remember, consumes the male.

Immediately after the outburst which follows Clarissa's sight of Miss Kilman and Elizabeth together, Clarissa sees the old lady in the house opposite, and is impressed by the solemnity of her separate existence, a solemnity which is compounded by her ignorance that she is being watched. 'Solemn' is a word that recurs frequently in *Mrs. Dalloway*, and it suggests an awe in the presence of another person, a self-effacing sense of personal smallness in the presence of a perceived separate identity which is to be respected as something *in and for itself*. This is why it is symbolically important that the old lady is not aware that she is being observed; her importance for Clarissa is not that the two of them have a relationship, but that they have an independence of each other:

> There was something solemn in it – but love and religion would destroy that, whatever it was, the privacy of the soul.
>
> (*MD* p. 140)

Love and religion share this demand to convert, to break down screens, which can be a positive process, but only when there is nothing self-regarding in it. Egocentricity and love together form a toxic combination.

It is egocentricity that pollutes Peter Walsh's love – both for Clarissa and Daisy:

> Love destroyed too. Everything that was fine, everything that was true went. Take Peter Walsh now. There was a man, charming, clever, with ideas about everything. If you wanted to know about Pope, say, or Addison, or just to talk nonsense, what people were like, what things meant, Peter knew better than anyone. . . . But look at the women he loved – vulgar, trivial, commonplace. Think of Peter in love – he came to see her after all these years, and what did he talk about? Himself. Horrible passion! she thought.
>
> (*MD* p. 140)

There is some confusion about Peter's precise relationship with Daisy, as he describes himself variously as in love for the first time, and as not in love with her. Whatever the case, it is certainly the egocentricity of his relationship with her that disgusts Clarissa, who presumably omits herself from the list of 'the women he loved'. It is because he wishes to impose his own identity on that of another person – he admits to himself that he is marrying Daisy primarily to stop anyone else marrying her – that he falls in love with women who are lacking in character and who cannot defend themselves against him. Whether or not this is to avoid a repetition of his disastrous relationship with Clarissa is hard to say. Peter Walsh is most to be admired when he talks (significantly) of those eighteenth-century authors whose very names conjure up an Augustan suspicion of the self and of private emotions. He is least to be admired when the experience of love releases his latent egocentricity.

Virginia Woolf sees love in complex, dialectical terms. Attempts to pin over simple labels on to the sexual desires or relationships of her character should be resisted. To argue that a particular character 'is' a lesbian, or that another character 'really' loves one person, is to fail to capture the complexity of her analysis of human sexual relationships. Her interest in androgyny, and her firm belief in the complementarity of masculine and feminine characteristics, should remind us that any discussion of sexuality in her novels should proceed with care and caution. However, it can be said that Virginia Woolf was interested in homosexuality, that many of her acquaintances were homosexual or bisexual in inclination, and that her interest and experience seem to be reflected in her fiction. There is, for example, a phrase in *Mrs. Dalloway* which describes Septimus and Evans as having been like 'two dogs on a hearthrug', which has a curious parallel in *Jacob's Room*. In this novel, which was written immediately before *Mrs. Dalloway*, the relationship between Jacob and Bonamy – who is described in such a way as to make it unambiguously clear that he is a homosexual – is referred to in the following way:

> Magnanimity, virtue – such words when Jacob used them in talk with Bonamy meant that he took control of the situation; that Bonamy would play round him like an affectionate spaniel; and that (as likely as not) they would end by rolling on the floor.

> (*JR* p. 164)

It might be deduced from this parallel that Septimus's inability to feel stems in part from an unconscious desire to suppress his homosexual feelings for Evans, which might also explain his

49

eagerness to get married to Rezia. Certainly, we are told that he develops 'manliness' in the war. But against this we need to set the fact that the recurrent references to dogs throughout *Mrs. Dalloway* seem to refer not so much to homosexuality, as to all open and loving emotional relationships.

Peter Walsh's love for Clarissa was one that, if allowed to develop, could have destroyed both of them. Her rejection of him, however, although in one sense it was necessary, may also have left a gap in the lives of both of them as a result of which each has been rendered incomplete. An absence of love in the character of Sir William Bradshaw is as emotionally crippling for him as is Peter Walsh's surfeit of the same unstable emotion. Near the close of the novel Clarissa, full of the news of Septimus's death, muses about both him and Sir William Bradshaw:

> Or there were the poets and thinkers. Suppose he [Septimus] had had that passion, and had gone to Sir William Bradshaw, a great doctor, yet to her obscurely evil, *without sex or lust*, extremely polite to women, but capable of some indescribable outrage – forcing your soul, that was it . . .
>
> (*MD* p. 203, my emphasis)

That 'without sex or lust' surely strikes an unexpected note. We expect 'obscurely evil' middle-aged men to have concealed reserves of secret sex and lust, to be like Hugh Whitbread, surprised into an apparently unrepresentative sexual advance like his kissing of Sally Seton. This absence in Sir William Bradshaw represents an absence of any desire for another person as another person; he is interested only in forcing other people's souls, imposing himself, egocentrically, on them. His lack of sex and love brings him, paradoxically, to that same blundering lack of respect for others that is fostered in Peter Walsh by love. Both an overwhelming love and a complete absence of sexuality can lead to a failure to perceive that 'together and apartness' of other people so necessary to fulfilling relationships.

The complexity that we find in the treatment of love in *Mrs. Dalloway* is not just an 'internal' matter, but relates to the relationships between love and other problems which the novel examines. It has been said that *Mrs. Dalloway* is weakened by the presentation of Sir William Bradshaw, who is 'turned into a caricature' and:

. . . even though he may not be exemplary in his private life, cannot and what is more does not, *qua* doctor, the doctor he is shown to be in the book, embody all the operations and noxious elements Mrs. Woolf would like to burden him with. Septimus's insanity was caused by the war and for that Dr. Bradshaw was not responsible, but Mrs. Woolf seems to imply that he was.[19]

The distinction between public and private life that is advanced here is, surely, precisely the sort of distinction that Virginia Woolf saw accepted in her society, but of which she was deeply suspicious. Both as a husband and as a doctor, Sir William Bradshaw lacks that respect for the separateness of other people, for the integrity of their souls, that Virginia Woolf not only sees as culpable, but which she sees as much behind the War as behind Sir William's treatment of Septimus. Sir William's association with the negative qualities of masculine egocentricity embodied in the state which he supports is also, in the symbolic context of *Mrs. Dalloway,* an association with the lack of love that made the war possible. Both Sir William Bradshaw and Hugh Whitbread have marriages based on repression and domination, and both are associated with the trappings of authority associated with the state, although Mrs Hugh has not quite 'gone under' as has Lady Bradshaw, and can still say something sharp (or cutting?). Septimus's experience of Sir William Bradshaw is a continuation of his experience of the war: the same lovelessness and lack of respect for human privacy characterise both.

It is consuming passion of which Virginia Woolf disapproves – because it consumes. E. M. Forster pointed out that the scenes in her novels concerned with eating are invariably good, and ingestion seems to offer her an effective objective correlative for certain human characteristics which she finds fascinating. Both Leonard Woolf and Quentin Bell have commented on the disgust at eating that accompanied her bouts of madness, which is perhaps reflected in Septimus's association with Shakespeare's disgust at 'the sordidity of the mouth and the belly'. It certainly seems noteworthy that both Miss Kilman and Hugh Whitbread are gluttons, and their appetite for food parallels their appetite for people, for a desire to consume the separateness of other people. Miss Kilman, unable to devour Elizabeth gorges on sticky chocolate eclairs.[20] It is surely no accident that it is a *pink* cake that Miss Kilman wants (and is deprived of), after both Elizabeth and Clarissa have been associated with this colour throughout the novel (although Clarissa is white after her illness). Miss Kilman, like Ellie Henderson, consumes but never gives.

Miss Kilman and Sir William Bradshaw have to be seen not quite as caricatures, but more as characters who carry a heavier symbolic function in the novel than, say, Peter Walsh, who is more of an 'independent' and complex character than they are. Thus in spite of the consuming nature of his love for Clarissa, we can note that, in his hotel, he is seen to address his food 'not gluttonously'. Although his love would have devoured Clarissa (and perhaps himself too) had they married, this is a result not of anything intrinsic to his character, but of something released or created in the particular relationship with Clarissa. We can refer to a marginal comment of Virginia Woolf's about this relationship:

> (A theory that certain people are so close that they infringe each other's independence – reason why she hadn't married Peter.)[21]

Clarissa had to break with Peter, 'or they would have been destroyed, both of them ruined', but for this neither is directly culpable. Love can reveal the differences between us; but if it reveals that there are too few differences, if we get too close to the loved one, then a relationship can become destructive as it can deny the separateness of each partner. Peter Walsh, thinking back to Bourton, remembers that 'They went in and out of each other's minds without any effort',[22] and Clarissa feels that with Peter 'everything had to be shared; everything gone into', and that includes, we suspect, each other's privacy, each other's independence.

Clarissa's relationship with Richard is different from this. Their independence of each other allows the relationship to flourish in a way that the relationship with Peter Walsh could not; it confirms each in his or her separate identity. Richard can tell Clarissa not to be a fool when he is bandaging her dog's paw –

That was what she liked him for, perhaps – that was what she needed.

(MD p. 83)

She certainly needs this more than a man like Peter Walsh who bursts into tears in her presence as his own pride, independence, identity even dissolve in front of her:

> And there is a dignity in people; a solitude; even between husband and wife a gulf; and that one must respect, thought Clarissa, watching him [Richard] open the door; for one would not part with it oneself, or take it, against his will, from one's husband, without losing one's independence, one's self-respect . . .

(MD p. 132)

The relationship between a respect for others and for oneself could not be more clearly stated. Richard's ability to help Clarissa depends upon his being separate from her, respecting her as an independent person:

> Even now, quite often if Richard had not been there reading the *Times*, so that she could crouch like a bird and gradually revive, send roaring up that immeasurable delight, rubbing stick to stick, one thing with another, she must have perished.

(MD p. 203)

'Stick', 'thing' – unusual words to describe a rich and satisfying relationship. Yet the inanimate quality of the images used does emphasise that important separateness which, paradoxically, is seen to be the necessary precondition of a fulfilling relationship. *The Times*, that symbol of masculine order and division, here represents a positive quality, as the screens are not in the excess but are preserving that dignity between husband and wife impossible when they go in and out of each other's minds.

This is not to say that the relationship between Richard and Clarissa is an ideal one. Her decision to reject Peter Walsh and to marry Richard was a necessary one for Clarissa, we feel. Yet *Mrs. Dalloway* constantly forces us to appreciate the strength of Johnson's point that one cannot simultaneously fill one's cup from the source and the end of the Nile: any such decision will involve gains and losses. Clarissa's rejection of Peter has, he claims, 'spoilt his life', and it has also left an absence in hers.

Returning home early in the novel, Clarissa is described as being 'Like a nun withdrawing, or a child exploring a tower', and the latter phrase is picked up later as an insistent child-hood memory of isolation – which may explain why Clarissa's progress up the stairs of her house is consistently seen as one towards privacy and isolation:

> It was all over for her. The sheet was stretched and the bed narrow. She had gone up into the tower alone and left them blackberrying in the sun.

(*MD* p. 52)

The sun, suggestive of openness and human contact, is left for the solitary room: on an earlier occasion Clarissa had felt that there was '. . . an emptiness about the heart of life; an attic room.' Now she actually sleeps in an attic room, ostensibly so that Richard, after all-night parliamentary sittings, will not disturb her. In fact we discover that:

> . . . really she preferred to read of the retreat from Moscow. He knew it. So the room was an attic; the bed narrow; and lying there reading, for she slept badly, she could not dispel a virginity preserved through childbirth which clung to her like a sheet. Lovely in girlhood, suddenly there came a moment – for example on the river beneath the woods at Clievedon – when, through some contraction of this cold spirit, she had failed him. And then at Constantinople, and again and again. She could see what she lacked. It was not beauty; it was not mind. It was something central which permeated; something warm which broke up surfaces and rippled the cold contact of men and women, or of women together.

(*MD* pp. 35, 36)

Clarissa's repudiation of sex, it has been said, is a repudiation of the life-force, and Peter Walsh is perhaps correct to date the death of the soul from that moment of prudishness when she left the table in embarrassment at Sally Seton's 'daring' re-mark.[23] It is as if defending her soul from intrusion has led to its at least partial death. That 'something central which perme-

54

ated' – a firm sense of autonomous identity that yet makes contact with other identities – has died in seclusion. The well-known dangers of biographical criticism should warn against any facile relating of Clarissa to Virginia Woolf herself, and yet we have the writer's own word for the fact that Clarissa is half herself, and parallels between Clarissa and Virginia Woolf are hard to avoid. Both were married to men interested in politics, and Nigel Nicolson's account of his parents' wandering fancies includes a letter from Vita Sackville-West to Harold Nicolson in which she admits that she had gone to bed twice with Virginia Woolf, and that, Virginia 'has never lived with anyone except Leonard, which was a terrible failure, and abandoned quite soon'.[24]

Later on in the novel, at three o'clock in the morning, Clarissa thinks of Elizabeth's relationship with Miss Kilman, and re-assures herself with the thought that 'it proves she has a heart'. Is there perhaps a suggestion that Clarissa wonders if she herself still has? This lack of hers is on rare occasions dissipated by her yielding to '. . . .the charm of a woman, not a girl, confessing, as to her they often did, some scrape, some folly'. 'Scraping' images in *Mrs. Dalloway*, which involve the severing of skin, the bringing together of surfaces, abound,[25] but for Clarissa this experience of contact is only vicarious. It is, however, presented very powerfully in terms of heterosexual physical passion:

It was a sudden revelation, a tinge like a blush which one tried to check and then, as it spread, one yielded to its expansion, and rushed to the farthest verge and there quivered and felt the world come closer, swollen with some astonishing significance, some pressure of rapture, which split its thin skin and gushed and poured with an extraordinary alleviation over the cracks and sores. Then, for that moment, she had seen an illumination; a match burning in a crocus; an inner meaning almost expressed. But the close withdrew; the hard softened. It was over – the moment.

(*MD* p. 36)

So forceful is this sensuous evocation of physical passion – tumescence, ejaculation and detumescence – that it is easy to forget that it is experienced by Clarissa through vicarious participation in another woman's recounted 'scrape'. Thus Clarissa is allowed to feel 'what men felt', but with no sexual demand being made on her – she has taken, but not given, and this is surely why she lacks 'something central which permeated', which can be possessed by someone who is prepared to *be* permeated. Clarissa feels, on looking back, that her feeling for Sally Seton was pure and had an integrity unlike a feeling for a man, because it was disinterested. Is it perhaps that another woman could make no sexual demand on her that allows Clarissa to feel more open to Sally Seton than to Richard or Peter Walsh? The young Sally Seton is described in masculine terms as a virile lover, picking flowers in a manner suggestive of the taking of virginity,[26] and immediately prior to her kissing Clarissa she also picks a flower. But the symbol is hollow; Sally Seton cannot take Clarissa's virginity, and even after childbirth Clarissa cannot dispel a virginity that clings to her like a sheet. She has never *given* herself fully in a sexual relationship, and her self is consequently impoverished.

Whereas Clarissa needs people, 'always people', Peter Walsh at one point in the novel concludes that he 'scarcely needed people any more', and he realises that his relationship with Daisy is pleasanter than his relationship with Clarissa because he is *not* in love with her, although she is in love with him. He thus receives that confirmation of self that contact with another person brings, without ever having to commit himself. A phrase associated with Peter Walsh throughout the novel is 'making up'. After trailing a pretty girl through London, he realises that:

> . . . it was smashed to atoms – his fun, for it was half made up, as he knew very well; invented, this escapade with the girl; made up, as one makes up the better part of life, he thought – making oneself up; making her up; creating an exquisite amusement, and something more. But odd it was, and quite true; all this one could never share . . .
>
> (*MD* p. 61)

Whether the 'better part of life' is the major, or the preferable part, is left ambiguous, but if the latter the question that the passage leaves the reader with is 'to whom?'. If this sort of experience cannot be shared, isn't it by definition a rather pale

56

shadow of what human contact of a real sort can bring? There is half a suggestion that Peter prefers his fantasies to real relationships. Clarissa too is guilty of 'making it up, building it round one, tumbling it . . .', and Peter advances the hypothesis that her parties are not so much for Richard, as for her idea of him – which we assume she has made up. It is certainly true that the reality of Miss Kilman and Clarissa's 'idea' of her are constantly juxtaposed in the novel. It seems as if the isolation that both Peter Walsh and Clarissa are forced into after their separation makes it necessary for both to make up experiences which they will never have:

> She shut the door. At once he became extremely depressed. It all seemed useless – going on being in love; going on quarrelling; going on making it up, and he wandered off alone . . .
>
> *(MD* p. 67)

'Making it up' is ambiguous here, and may just refer to repairing a relationship. But Peter Walsh and Clarissa never seem to be able to achieve a balanced relationship such as Richard and Clarissa enjoy. When Peter visits Clarissa, years later, he bursts into her room in domineering masculine fashion, while she makes 'to hide her dress, like a virgin protecting chastity, respecting privacy', but shortly after this he has burst into tears. He either seeks to impose himself forcibly on her, or he dissolves before her. They are perpetually incapable of reaching that equilibrium of 'together and apartness' that Clarissa and Richard succeed in establishing.

In his biography of Virginia Woolf Quentin Bell quotes from a letter written by her around June 1906 to Madge Vaughan (née Symonds), who, according to Vita Sackville-West, 'is Sally in *Mrs Dalloway*'. (*VWABI* p. 61).

> But my present feeling is that this vague & dream like world, without love, or heart, or passion, or sex, is the world I really care about, & find interesting. For, though they are dreams to you, & I cant express them at all adequately, these things are perfectly real to me.
>
> *(VWABI* p. 126)

If we think of this 'vague and dream like world' as a state in which only fantasy experiences are indulged in, we can see why it lacks love, heart, passion and sex. All of these can only be indulged in *socially*, with (at least) two people experiencing them together. We know that Clarissa is no longer sleeping with Richard, either literally or metaphorically; we know too that she cannot understand passion, speaks slightingly of love, and is relieved to find that Elizabeth is capable of affection and 'has a heart' — even if Miss Kilman is in possession of it. Is it not possible that Clarissa, like Peter Walsh, has made up too much of her experience with the opposite sex, and has found that although fantasies are conveniently manipulable, they do not provide 'something warm which broke up surfaces and rippled together the cold contact of men and women'? In fact the reason why 'making up' is an alluring pastime is that it can be indulged in with no danger to 'surfaces', to one's screens; but unless one's surfaces are repeatedly broken up and re-formed, one's 'inner-oyster' atrophies and that 'something central which permeated' is lost. In choosing to 'make up' life rather than to live it Peter Walsh — and perhaps Clarissa too — has endangered the very thing he has been concerned to protect.

The distinction between fantasy and imagination tends to be a quantitative rather than a qualitative one. If we feel that some-one lives too much in the here-and-now, rarely putting him-self imaginatively into different situations, then we call him unimaginative. If, on the other hand, he copes with problems in the here-and-now only by escaping to imaginative states which do not affect his behaviour in the present at all, then we tend to characterise these states as fantasies. Perhaps the crucial distinction is whether the imaginative or fantasy state is com-pletely self-enclosed and cut-off from the here-and-now situa-tion, or whether the individual tacks between the two in a manner comparable to that alternation between privacy and communion which Virginia Woolf sees as basic to the creative process. It is revealing that although Peter Walsh is associated with the term 'making up' throughout the novel, in the early stages of Clarissa's party she considers him to be culpable for his inability to risk his 'one little point of view'. In other words, there is an association between indulgence in the relief that fantasy brings, and an inability or unwillingness to put oneself into the position of another real person. The characters who people our fantasies are not 'there', they are puppets manipulated by ourselves, and unless we indulge in real human contact so as to expose their insufficiency, we become used to having no real pressure put on us to modify the way we see the world and other people. It is a measure of the success of Clarissa's party that it forces Peter Walsh out of his 'making up' habit into actually perceiving the reality of another person.

The persona of Blake's poem 'The Angel' dreams that he or she is a maiden queen who hides from her guardian angel her 'heart's delight':

> So he took his wings and fled;
> Then the morn blush'd rosy red;
> I dried my tears, & arm'd my fears
> With ten thousand shields and spears.
>
> Soon my Angel came again:
> I was arm'd, he came in vain;
> For the time of youth was fled,
> And grey hairs were on my head.

Grey is a sinister colour in *Mrs. Dalloway*. It is the colour of the blind of the official car, of Sir William Bradshaw's car and of his room. We also learn that both Clarissa and Peter Walsh are now grey haired, and the latter is described as 'a man in grey' by Septimus. It seems possible that Clarissa's preference for her attic room, and Peter's preference for 'making up' are both examples of hiding 'the heart's delight' from others, an action which leads both to 'arm their fears with ten thousand shields and spears', so that when Peter Walsh comes back, he comes in vain.

Virginia Woolf frequently expressed her admiration for the writing of Laurence Sterne, and this is not surprising. Sterne understood about arming one's fears. In *Tristram Shandy* Uncle Toby goes straight from convalescence in bed to indulgence of his hobby-horse, and his military obsessions act as a screen which protects him from the intrusion of unwelcome forces. Sterne's characters are all very much aware of the need to protect their dreams – although we are not surprised that it is sexuality in the form of Trim's carnal lusts that breaks down poor Toby's hobby-horsical fortifications. In spite of this ability that his characters have to live secure in their own world, they manage to communicate with one another to a surprising degree, and this combination of ontological security and satisfactory communication with others must have seemed to Virginia Woolf very close to her own ideal of a secure sense of personal identity which did not preclude full and open communication with others. When, in *Tristram Shandy*, Toby covers his confusion at an indirect allusion to sexual indiscretion made by his brother Walter by whistling Lillibulero, his brother is able to understand that he is embarrassed. Toby and his brother are like Clarissa and Peter, who 'always had this queer power of communicating without words'. This is not to say that Clarissa rejects language as a means of communication, however. Regretting the failure of the young people at her party to talk, Clarissa calls to mind 'the enormous resources of the English language', and the power it bestows 'of communicating feelings', and ponders on the fact that at their age 'she and Peter would have been arguing all the evening'.

This insistence on the power of language notwithstanding, it is fair to say that the supreme moments of communication and contact in the novel are not verbal. Richard cannot bring himself to tell Clarissa that he loves her in words, but he gives her roses, symbolising those 'moments' of exultation and communion so important to Virginia Woolf. He has, significantly, been carrying the flowers 'like a weapon', and his gift of the flowers to Clarissa seems to suggest that he is possessed of the feminine ability to throw away what Blake calls 'shields and spears', an ability that contrasts with Peter's oscillation between less controlled extremes of aggression and dissolution. It is Richard who, alternating between that independence symbolised in his reading of *The Times* and the self-exposure symbolised in his giving up of his 'weapon', offers us the nearest to a Woolfian ideal of 'together and apartness' in *Mrs. Dalloway*. Clarissa's acceptance of vulnerability seems to be limited to the giving of parties.

In spite of Richard's ability to accept an emotional vulnerability in his relationship with Clarissa that Clarissa herself finds impossible, Virginia Woolf seems to have considered this ability to 'open oneself', to accept danger and vulnerability, as more a feminine than a masculine characteristic. It is significant that when Peter Walsh speaks to Clarissa after she has been kissed by Sally Seton, 'It was like running one's face against a granite wall in the darkness!' Both Peter Walsh and (the older) Sally Seton are described as being egotistic, but Sally's egotism is, 'the most *open* desire to be thought first always' (my emphasis), whereas Peter Walsh's egotism is associated with walls, boundaries, divisions, and we are not surprised to learn that he detests the moon, that symbol of a feminine ability to soften outlines and destroy dividing lines. On the other hand, it is Peter Walsh's look of 'having reserves' that makes him attractive to women, '. . . who liked the sense that he was not altogether manly', a judgement confirmed for the reader by Peter's bursting into tears in Clarissa's presence. It is in the trenches that Septimus develops 'manliness', which dries up his 'feminine' ability to communicate freely and openly, and has the same ultimate effect on him as is seen in the boy soldiers Peter Walsh observes drilling in London:

> . . . as if one will worked legs and arms uniformly, and life, with its varieties, its irreticences, had been laid under a pavement of monuments and wreaths and drugged into a stiff yet staring corpse by discipline.
>
> (*MD* p. 57)

The devotee of *Catch 22* may recall that Lieutenant Scheisskopf, obsessed by the need to improve the drilling of his men, had considered nailing the twelve men in each rank to a long two-by-four beam of seasoned oak to keep them in line, and the contrast between this insane military desire for an order that will subdue life, and his wife's irrepressible carnal lusts, is not so far removed from the contrast between life and discipline that the above passage presents us with. The same masculine desire to impose order on life is seen in Sir William Bradshaw's 'proportion' as in the discipline of the army. We are not surprised to learn that although Peter Walsh has not, like Septimus, *stopped* feeling, he admits to not knowing what it is that he does feel.

Clarissa's relationship with Miss Kilman involves certain paradoxical elements which should not be overlooked at this point. We learn that:

. . . no doubt with another throw of the dice, had the black
been uppermost and not the white, she would have loved
Miss Kilman! But not in this world. No.

(*MD* p. 15)

The lady is perhaps protesting too much, for later on we find
that her relationship with Miss Kilman is not an absolutely
loveless one:

Ah, how she hated her – hot, hypocritical, corrupt; with all
that power; Elizabeth's seducer; the woman who had crept
in to steal and defile. . . . She hated her: she loved her. It was
enemies one wanted, not friends . . .

(*MD* p. 192)

R. D. Laing, in *The Divided Self*, suggests that to the schizophrenic, liking someone equals *being like* them, and threatens
loss of identity. He suggests that as a result, hating and being
hated may therefore seem preferable. It seems as if this may
partially explain Clarissa's attitude to Miss Kilman. If Miss
Kilman hates her, then it confirms her identity, suggests that
she is separate and distinct from Miss Kilman – even poses some
threat to the poor lady. For this privilege Clarissa is grateful,
and so she 'loves' Miss Kilman for the experience of hating that
she provides, which confirms her identity without demanding
that she make herself vulnerable, that she *give* anything. Receiving without giving alienates the receiver from the giver as
certainly in human sexual relationships as it does in social relationships based on economic exploitation, and Clarissa's lack
of something 'central which permeated' can be related to the
social and sexual parasitism of which she is guilty. This, to be
sure, is not the whole of Clarissa, but it is a significant and an
important part.

When Mrs Shandy, in *Tristram Shandy*, tells her husband
that Toby is going to get married, her husband's response is
one that gets to the heart of the matter: 'Then he will never . . .
be able to lie *diagonally* in his bed again as long as he lives.'
What seems to be wrong with Clarissa's relationships with men
is that the inability to lie diagonally in her bed – and all that
this implies in terms of accepting restrictions on her personal
freedom – is not something that she is prepared to accept.

62

One of the paradoxical experiences of love which *Mrs. Dalloway* explores is that of being brought closer to a person by being rejected by them. Rejection means that a clear distinction is drawn between two people, that the loved one is in one completely unambiguous sense *separate* from the person who has been rejected. Paradoxically, this can make the loved one more desirable, for their well-defined separateness has the effect of presenting the outlines of their distinct identity so much more clearly. I do not think that it is accidental that it is the rejected Peter Walsh rather than Richard or Sally who sees that Clarissa is 'there' at the end of the novel; because she has rejected him, in a sense cut herself off from him, her identity is more clearly defined for him than it is for Richard or for Sally. One of the paradoxes that *Mrs. Dalloway* leaves us with is that our perception of another person's unattainableness may be what draws us to them. Peter Walsh could not say that 'there she was' when the two of them were passing in and out of each other's minds, he can only say it when her separation from him defines her identity for him. He would not say 'there she was' of Daisy, for her love for him means that she is more 'here' than 'there', more part of him and thus possessed less of a discrete and separate identity.

Love, then, as Katharine Hilbery remarks in *Night and Day,* can stand for many different things, and yet all are unmistakable and not to be passed by. It can be seen in the song of the old woman Peter Walsh sees singing in the street with 'the voice of no age or sex', conquering time and the division of the human race into separate sexes. But it can threaten the privacy of the soul and resemble conversion in its desire to destroy human separateness and individuality. In a society where men and women can only be themselves by simultaneously co-operating and competing with their fellows, its central paradoxes and tensions offer a powerful symbolic illustration of the 'together and apartness' of human relationships.

# 5

# THE CHARTERED STREET

Then (as I was walking through Russell Square last night)
I see the mountains in the sky: the great clouds; and the
moon which is risen over Persia; I have a great and astonishing sense of something there, which is 'it'. It is not exactly
beauty that I mean. It is that the thing is in itself enough:
satisfactory; achieved. A sense of my own strangeness, walking on the earth is there too: of the infinite oddity of the
human position; trotting along Russell Square with the
moon up there and those mountain clouds. Who am I, what
am I, and so on: these questions are always floating about in
me: and then I bump against some exact fact – a letter, a
person, and come to them again with a great sense of fresh-
ness.
                                                    (*AWD* p. 86)

It is hard to imagine the above passage having been written by
anyone but Virginia Woolf. The vaguely mystical feeling of an
achieved 'moment', coupled with a searching after some satisfactory definition of her own identity, are characteristically
'Woolfian'. Whether or not deliberately, the omission of question marks from the two key questions – 'Who am I, what am I'
– gives a curiously disembodied, alienated effect to the words,
as if the question had to be asked, but, 'to whom?'[27] The passage comes from Virginia Woolf's diary, and was written the
year after the publication of *Mrs. Dalloway*. It offers ample
evidence to substantiate the claim that Clarissa's search for a
secure sense of self owed much to a similar quest on the part
of her creator. There is, however, one aspect of this passage
that is easy to miss, but which also seems to me to be highly
significant: the fact that it is 'set' in the streets of London. There
is something peculiarly appropriate in the fact that this sudden
need to search for a secure definition of her self should assail
Virginia Woolf at night and in Russell Square, and for the
reader of *Mrs. Dalloway* this setting has a very familiar ring.

There is, on the second page of the novel, a highly significant
and apparently casual comparison thrown out:

For having lived in Westminster – how many years now? over twenty, – one feels even in the midst of the traffic, or waking at night, Clarissa was positive, a particular hush, or solemnity; an indescribable pause; a suspense (but that might be her heart, affected, they said, by influenza) before Big Ben strikes.

(*MD* p. 6)

'in the midst of the traffic, or waking at night'; it is surely, an unusual juxtaposition. Yet the juxtaposition works, poetically, because both situations convey that sense of self-conscious isolation that the passage demands. The night cuts one off from people in a very simple sense: in the dark we can see little, and so are conscious more of ourselves. This phenomenon must have been far more marked even in Virginia Woolf's less well-lit London than it is today. This feeling of isolation and self-consciousness at night time is not difficult to understand. But 'in the midst of the traffic'? Raymond Williams has pointed out that the discontinuity and atomism of the city were aesthetically experienced by Virginia Woolf as a problem of perception which raised problems of identity, and he notes, commenting on a passage from *Orlando*, that these problems were characteristically resolved on arrival in the country.[28]

It is impossible to imagine the 'present' action of *Mrs. Dalloway* apart from the city, for the atmosphere of city life and its contrast with the countryside – Bourton in particular – of the characters' youth is a crucial element in the total effect of the novel. *Mrs. Dalloway* is probably not a novel that would spring to mind were one asked to name a 'London novel', perhaps because of the social restrictiveness of its viewpoint. One would be more likely to think of Dickens's fiction, in which a wider and seemingly more complete cross-section of London life is presented. And yet *Mrs. Dalloway* is saturated with references to London and is, in a very fundamental sense, a novel that is concerned with certain key aspects of the urban experience. Specific references to London places, streets, sights, activities and atmosphere recur throughout the novel, and nearly always at the time that we are following the *private* thoughts of one of the main characters. In the first two pages of the novel we have references to 'Rumpelmayer's men',

65

'Durtnall's van', 'Westminster' (twice), 'Big Ben', 'Victoria Street', 'Acts of Parliament', and 'London'. This is no mere pasting in of 'background', but is part of the central experience of the novel which continues throughout the book. Although the scene of action or contemplation moves about both historically and geographically to a considerable extent, at any given point in the novel the reader is nearly always able to pinpoint the exact location of what is happening with complete accuracy.

As I have suggested, this is not just a question of giving 'background' information. The sort of human experiences Virginia Woolf is concerned with are organically related to the experience of large city life. That sense of her own strangeness described by Virginia Woolf in the passage I quoted from her diary is part of that anonymity felt by the city dweller, whose relationships with other people are such as seem to stress his own separation from them. We cannot imagine Wemmick's two selves distributed in a reversed way between country and city; like Virginia Woolf, Dickens was aware that alienation belonged to the city, however much (as Raymond Williams has pointed out), it was a phenomenon that included the country in its effects. From Blake's 'London' to Eliot's 'Rhapsody on a Windy Night', the situation of a lonely wanderer in a city street has been *the* symbol of human alienation. Raymond Williams has commented on that paradoxical feeling of being alone in a crowded street, which he describes as the most written-about experience of city life, noting that the experience *is* paradoxical, because the city is, above all other places, the centre for exchange, communication and control.[29] It is the place where most people are, and yet where least human contact can seem to take place.

I would suggest that the experience is so much written about because it offers a perfect symbol of alienation, an experience fundamental to our society, but seen in its most extreme and naked form in the city. It is not so much that the city causes alienation but rather that a particular form of social structure encouraged the development of a set of social relationships in the city, which then offered themselves as the perfect symbol of that basic structure. The individual in our society, like the isolated individual in the city, is surrounded by people with whom he has to relate, to whom he has to communicate, but

66

who are essentially 'private', separate from him. It is, of course, precisely when our human contacts are at a superficial level that we start to ask ourselves who and what we are, because normal human contact is not answering the question for us.

I have already mentioned Virginia Woolf's admiration for Laurence Sterne, and as I said we do not find this admiration surprising: the two writers seem to have shared a similar interest in the minutiae of human perception and communcation which led both to initiate similar technical revolutions in the art of the novel, and Virginia Woolf must have recognised much of herself in Sterne. But Virginia Woolf also had a great admiration for a very different eighteenth-century novelist – Daniel Defoe – and this is not quite such an obvious literary affinity. Is not Defoe more the sort of novelist that Virginia Woolf's 'materialists' such as Bennett would have admired, with his unshakeable belief in the importance of 'things', and his treatment of friends and friendships as if they were possessions? Significantly, it is the Defoe of *Moll Flanders* that attracts and fascinates Virginia Woolf, and in 1919 she is writing in her diary that:

> These ten minutes are stolen from *Moll Flanders*, which I failed to finish yesterday in accordance with my time sheet, yielding to a desire to stop reading and go up to London. But I saw London, in particular the view of white city churches and palaces from Hungerford Bridge through the eyes of Defoe. . . . Yes, a great writer surely to be there imposing himself on me after 200 years.
>
> (*AWD* pp. 11, 12)

I would suggest that Defoe's London impresses Virginia Woolf so much because Defoe uses London – consciously or unconsciously – as a symbol of the social relations fundamental to his society. Moll Flanders's treatment of her friends, acquaintances, husbands, is artistically 'right' because it reflects both Defoe's concrete experience of London life, and also his artistic insight into the social relations which lay behind this experience. Moll, like Clarissa, is continually needing people to help her, but retains a privacy, a separateness – even from successive husbands – which is very similar to Clarissa's. *Moll Flanders* is full of characters who meet one another, communicate,

67

interrelate, even marry, but who never give up that privacy of the self that seems to be related to the burgeoning capitalism of the early eighteenth century. The reader of *Moll Flanders* finishes the novel with contradictory feelings: he has come near to one man's perception of the possibilities of human communion and solidarity, and yet fighting against this all the time he sees competitive individualism, greed and selfishness. To this extent, the novel reflects the same basic contradictions in Defoe's society that I have discussed earlier with reference to our own.

Septimus Smith, like Moll, undergoes those 'solitary experiences' which people 'go through alone, in their bedrooms, in their offices, walking the fields and the streets of London'. Unlike Moll, however, the protective refusal to feel which is his response to his alienation, destroys him. Septimus, like so many of the characters in *Mrs. Dalloway*, has come to London from outside – Stroud in his case. He has had great expectations – as had Dickens's Pip when he made a similar journey. But:

> London has swallowed up many millions of young men called Smith; thought nothing of fantastic Christian names like Septimus with which their parents have thought to distinguish them. Lodging off the Euston Road, there were experiences, again experiences, such as change a face in two years from a pink innocent oval to a face lean, contracted, hostile.
>
> (*MD* p. 94)

In an early draft of this passage Virginia Woolf used the word 'suspicious' to describe the change that London effects in Septimus.[30] Like Clarissa, he is seen to have lost that fresh pinkness that symbolises both youth and naturalness, and to have been changed by London into an *individualistic*, competitive person, locked in himself through distrust of others. Thus, as I have already argued, Septimus's war experiences are not to be seen as qualitatively new; his antagonism towards other men has been engendered in London by the competitive individualism that that city encourages in its members. The city that gives Clarissa a feeling of privacy in its streets is a product of the same forces that reduce Septimus to madness, and is an important element in his loss of contact with other people. London – like the war – offers itself as a perfect symbol of the contradictory human relationships in Virginia Woolf's society, with its disorientating blend of co-operation and competitiveness evident in so many of its characteristics.

One can point to the 'closed car' in *Mrs. Dalloway* as a potent symbol of this combination of surface co-operation and fundamental individualism and enclosure. (It is also, incidentally, one of a number of possible echoes of T. S. Eliot's early poetry that *Mrs. Dalloway* contains, a subject I want to touch on shortly.) Early on in the novel, the closed car, associated with the sinister colour grey which seems to represent a number of negative qualities including the disillusionment of age in *Mrs. Dalloway*, stops outside the florists within which Clarissa is buying flowers. It contains an important human being, that much people outside know, but a male hand (of course!) draws the blind, and the screen-making habit has cut off the important person from those all around him. The car is a potent symbol here for a number of reasons. The development of motor transport – especially in cities – is very intimately related to the social relationships that our society rests upon. Raymond Williams has some penetrating remarks to make on this subject in his *The Country and the City*:

> It is impossible to read the early descriptions of crowded metropolitan streets – the people as isolated atoms, flowing this way and that; a common stream of separated identities and directions – without seeing, past them, this mode of relationship embodied in the modern car: private, enclosed, an individual vehicle in a pressing and merely aggregated common flow; certain underlying conventions of external control but within them the passing of rapid signals of warning, avoidance, concession, irritation, as we pursue our ultimately separate ways but in a common mode.

This seems to me to be a brilliant insight into the way a particular social phenomenon can encapsulate the contradictions inherent in the society which gives rise to it: 'merely aggregated common flow' is just right – as I have suggested earlier, it implies an order which ignores microscopic phenomena, in this case human individuality. One parallel between motor transport and the human relationships that give rise to it that Williams does not mention is the common occurrence of a large number of accidents – of which Septimus's fate is an apt reminder.

I suspect that we are meant to presume that the passenger in the closed car may be the Prime Minister, who appears later on at Clarissa's party. The closed car and the Prime Minister are described as, respectively, a symbol of the state and a symbol of English society, and the word 'majesty' recurs in both scenes. But, of course, the reader is in exactly the same position as the bystander in the street; he cannot be sure who is in the car, and it is this unsureness that stands as a fitting symbol of the state, a state where people do pass one another without making any real, human contact. We are not surprised to learn that Sir William Bradshaw, that other loyal supporter of the state, also possesses a grey car. In this way Virginia Woolf makes a more or less explicit identification between the lack of contact between people in the novel and the society to which they belong. The secrecy of the closed car is seen in exaggerated form in the secrecy of the ambulance that carries Septimus's body away, and which Peter Walsh sees – correctly – as representative of English 'civilisation'. In death, as in life, civilisation has hidden the real Septimus from those all around him.

It is probable that there were especially painful reasons why London should offer itself to Virginia Woolf as a powerful and rich symbol of human alienation. In *Beginning Again,* Leonard Woolf noted that his wife was unable to walk in the street anywhere without people stopping, staring at her, and nudging one another to look at her. People, he says, found her appearance somehow ridiculous, and he suggests that this was partly because she seemed to be 'thinking of something else', 'shuffling along the streets in the shadow of a dream' – in other words, carrying the anonymity of the street a stage further than was normal. Not surprisingly, she was extremely distressed by this sort of experience; in *Night and Day* we are told that passers-by thought Katharine Hilbery 'reprehensibly and almost ridiculously detached from the surrounding scene':

> But her beauty saved her from the worst fate that can befall a pedestrian; people looked at her, but they did not laugh.
>
> (*NAD* p. 331)

Virginia Woolf had, Leonard Woolf tells us, a horror of being stared at or photographed, and her private horrors would seem to have been incorporated into Septimus's sense of persecution in the street:

> It is I who am blocking the way, he thought. Was he not being looked at and pointed at; was he not weighted there, rooted to the pavement, for a purpose? . . .
> People must notice; people must see. People, she [Rezia] thought, looking at the crowd staring at the motor car . . .
> (MD p. 18)

*causes Alienation*

Virginia Woolf certainly seems to have had a highly ambivalent attitude towards London, which seems to have been related to the fact that the city appeared to offer both anonymity and isolation. During her illness in 1921 and 1922 she had been taken away to the quiet of Richmond (and, interestingly, had been prevented from attending parties), but as she got better she longed to return to the city. According to Quentin Bell the early bouts of madness that Virginia Woolf experienced towards the end of the nineteenth century were accompanied by a fear of facing strangers in the street. Bell relates this to her having seen – or having claimed to have seen – a number of street accidents. Yet in spite of this she was apparently fascinated by the experience of wandering alone in a city street, an experience which seemed at times to give her a sense of personal privacy in the midst of human contact that can perhaps be compared to Clarissa's feelings on seeing the old lady in the room opposite.

In her essay 'Street Haunting' Virginia Woolf describes the experience of leaving one's home for the city street in the following terms:

> . . . we shed the self our friends know us by and become part of that vast republican army of anonymous trampers, whose society is so agreeable after the solitude of one's own room.
> (CE4 p. 155)

For Clarissa, it would seem that the company of other, anonymous people satisfies her need for human contact without making demands on her which she feels would threaten her ontological security. Interestingly enough, 'Street Haunting' associates the word 'dally' with the activity described by its title, which may throw some light on the significance of Clarissa's name – one she adopts after 'Parry-ing' Peter Walsh. In the essay the narrator at one stage encounters a dwarf who draws to herself the attention that, it would appear, Virginia Woolf habitually attracted to herself in the street. The dwarf appears to call into being an atmosphere which actually creates 'the humped, the twisted, the deformed'. Human deformity of course draws attention to the particularity, the individuality of people, who can no longer be regarded as a 'vast republican army'. It is significant that whereas Peter Walsh sees boy *soldiers* drilling in the streets – the many reduced to uniformity – Septimus meets with a very different spectacle of a group of people in which human particularity is garishly exaggerated:

> In the streets, vans roared past him; brutality blared out on placards; men were trapped in mines; women burnt alive; and once a maimed file of lunatics being exercised or displayed for the diversion of the populace (who laughed aloud) ambled and nodded and grinned past him, in the Tottenham Court Road, each half apologetically, yet triumphantly, inflicting his hopeless woe. And would *he* go mad?
>
> (*MD* p. 100)

It is interesting to compare this passage both with Doris Lessing's *The Golden Notebook*, where the experience of madness and isolation is accompanied by an increasing fascinated horror at 'News' of human tragedy on an almost unimaginable scale, and with Sylvia Plath's poems in *Ariel*, where again private alienation and horror are fused with an obsessive concern at large-scale acts of brutality. Plath's poem 'Berck Plage' also introduces a group of crippled individuals along with a subjective feeling of horrified disengagement, and it would seem that for Sylvia Plath as for Virginia Woolf deformity appears to be an appropriate objective correlative for the subjective experience of being imprisoned in one's self.

I have already mentioned 'Rhapsody on a Windy Night', and more detailed consideration of the influence on *Mrs. Dalloway* of Eliot's poetry seems now to be appropriate. The Woolfs had printed and published *Poems* in 1920, and they knew Eliot personally and as a poet. Dorothy Brewster, in her *Virginia Woolf's London*, argues that

The crowds streaming incessantly back and forth over Waterloo and Westminster and London Bridge are not those of Mr Eliot's Unreal City – death has not undone them in six hundred years.[31]

And yet Peter Walsh sees the leaves in the square as 'the foliage of some submerged city', and my own feeling is that the London of *Mrs. Dalloway* is in many respects very close to Mr Eliot's Unreal City. I have already referred to the image of the closed car – which can be found in the second section of 'The Waste Land' – and in the same poem we find a reference to the 'dead sound on the final stroke of nine' in 'The Burial of the Dead', which the following passage brings strongly to mind:

> It was her heart, he remembered; and the sudden loudness of the final stroke tolled for death that surprised in the midst of life, Clarissa falling where she stood, in her drawing-room. No! No! he cried. She is not dead! I am not old ...
>
> (*MD* p. 56)

The fact that Septimus, like the persona of 'Gerontion', who has lost his sight, smell, hearing taste and touch, can neither taste nor feel, points to a concern with the loss of sensory contact with the world which is common to both writers. Similarly, the disgust at sex with which Eliot's early poetry is permeated is paralleled by Septimus's perception of a similar repulsion in Shakespeare. Early on in *Mrs. Dalloway* we have a description of motor engines whose throb, 'sounded like a pulse irregularly drumming through an entire body', which recalls the human engine in the third section of 'The Waste Land', which waits like a taxi, throbbing, and the drowned sailor, to whom Septimus compares himself, can be related to the symbol of the fertility god in the same poem.[32]

Now searching for literary echoes can be a dull and sterile business: we should have in our minds the awful warning of Charles Tansley in *To the Lighthouse*, writing his thesis on the influence of something upon somebody and unable to absorb the beneficent influences all around him. But it does seem to me to be of importance to stress that both Virginia Woolf and T. S. Eliot see certain characteristics of London to be representative of a deeper inadequacy in their time. Septimus's refusal to have children, like the reference to abortion and contraception in 'The Waste Land', ties in with the general feeling that there has been an artificial stifling of the springs of human fruitfulness and fecundity that we find both in 'The Waste Land' and in *Mrs. Dalloway*. If it is correct to see Septimus as symbolically analogous to the drowned sailor of the fertility myth, then it is possible that his death is to be seen as a necessary prelude to the releasing of the powers of rebirth in Clarissa and in her party.

In her essay 'Gas', Virginia Woolf states that all the faces seen in the third-class railway carriage belonging to those more than twenty years old appear to have been under gas, and there is a sense in which both Clarissa and Septimus seem like patients etherised upon a table, cut off from other people. It is certainly true that for both Virginia Woolf and T. S. Eliot the position of the individual in the London street is a contemplative one: like Prufrock, Clarissa, Peter Walsh and Septimus are all observers of, rather than participators in life.

I have suggested that Virginia Woolf's attitude to London was an ambivalent one, and that the experience of different characters in *Mrs. Dalloway* in the London streets reveals different aspects of this ambivalence, and of the social contradictions that seem to underly it. The London street can offer a stimulating privacy in which the individual's fantasy can have full play, or a deadening isolation in which the individual feels vulnerable and abandoned. For Peter Walsh, who knows no one there, the experience of being in London makes the earth seem like an island:

> ... the strangeness of standing alone, alive, unknown, at half-past eleven in Trafalgar Square overcame him. What is it? Where am I?
>
> (*MD* p. 58)

The passage describing this strange mélange of feelings ends with the words, 'He had not felt so young for years.' The escape from his human relations with Daisy – and even Clarissa – into the anonymity of London makes him feel young and, as we see soon after, free. For Septimus, who doesn't carry with him the identity-confirming knowledge that he is loved, the experience is very different:

He looked at people outside; happy they seemed, collecting in the middle of the street, shouting, laughing, squabbling over nothing. But he could not taste, he could not feel. In the tea-shop among the tables and the chattering waiters the appalling fear came over him – he could not feel.

(*MD* pp. 97, 98)

With some possible justification he concludes that, 'it must be the fault of the world then – that he could not feel'. Septimus's lack of feeling indicates a general deadness in society in a machine age, the same deadness that Eliot is concerned to explore in 'The Waste Land'.[33]

The ambivalence that Virginia Woolf reveals in her attitude to London is partly a matter of the contradictions inherent in the society it reflects, but partly also a matter of her more general ambivalence about 'screens' and the way in which they can both protect and destroy. One of the most fascinating, and historically recent experiences of city life, is that of being terribly close to other people, people one knows, yet somehow missing them. The relationship between Clarissa and Septimus – if we can accurately talk of a relationship between the two in other than literary terms – is curiously similar in many ways to this recurrent city experience. Although they never actually meet, Clarissa learns of Septimus through the medium of Sir William Bradshaw, and through this indirect contact she is brought to feel that she understands his reason for killing himself. A letter written by Virginia Woolf (then Virginia Stephen) to Violet Dickinson in or around 1903 contains a suggestive and relevant passage:

I'm going to have a man and a woman – show them growing up – never meeting – not knowing each other – but all the time you'll feel them come nearer and nearer. This will be the real exciting part (as you see) – but when they almost meet – only a door between – you see how they just miss – and go off at a tangent, and never come anywhere near again.

(*VWA Bl* p. 125)

Quentin Bell notes that the play outlined above was in fact never written, but we need only think of certain potential but unrealised relationships in *Mrs. Dalloway* to become aware of the fact that although the idea of the play may have been dropped, aspects of it were to reappear in *Mrs. Dalloway*.

If we wish to understand the fascination of this 'nearly-meeting-but-not-quite' theme, we need to see it in the context of the whole complex net of human relationships that the nine-teenth and twentieth century city dweller found him or herself involved in. Another writer whose work Virginia Woolf much admired was Thomas De Quincey, and in his *The Confessions of an English Opium Eater* we find De Quincey musing about the young prostitute Ann,[34] with whom he had discovered some human contact, but who had slipped out of his life after a while:

> If she lived, doubtless we must have been sometimes in search of each other, at the very moment, through the mighty laby-rinths of London; perhaps even within a few feet of each other – a barrier no wider, in a London street, often amount-ing in the end to a separation for eternity!

Doubtless this situation appealed to De Quincey's curiosity partly because of its historical novelty: we need to remember that the state of affairs he hypothesises must occur only very infrequently in small rural communities. But, on a more funda-mental level, it seems that the situation fascinates him because it somehow symbolises the sort of human relationships that his London encourages and allows, based on nearness and osten-sible contact, but in fact allowing little real human recognition.

In *Mrs. Dalloway* a situation very similar to the one De Quincey imagines is described:

> The face itself had been seen only once by three people for a few seconds. Even the sex was now in dispute. But there could be no doubt that greatness was seated within; greatness was passing, hidden, down Bond Street, removed only by a hand's-breadth from ordinary people who might now, for the first time and last, be within speaking distance of the majesty of England, of the enduring symbol of the state . . .
>
> (*MD* p. 19)

It is fitting that a state based on a system which allows human communion on one level (the production of wealth) but denies it on another (the ownership of wealth) should be symbolised by the anonymous yet known figure in the car, removed

76

from ordinary people by a hand's-breadth which, in **De Quincey**'s words, amounted 'in the end to a separation for eternity'.

Mention of De Quincey brings to mind a common element in his work and that of T. S. Eliot – the drugged state, in which fantasy and reality become indistinguishable. In an alienated situation, unable to communicate with other people, individuals have resort to fantasy-experiences and are subject to hallucinations. Unable to cope with the impersonality of London, De Quincey hurries through the streets full of people to consume the opium that is to compensate for the inadequacies of his life. Mr Verloc, in *The Secret Agent* sells fantasy in the form of pornography, still to be found in its most blatant form in central London today. I have already commented on the recurrent association of the phrase 'making up' with Peter Walsh in *Mrs. Dalloway*. Peter Walsh's pursuit of the pretty but unknown girl through the streets of London leads to his making up a complicated fantasy relationship with her. 'One doesn't want people after fifty', but he must have his dreams. After hearing the bell of the ambulance which carries Septimus's body, Peter Walsh is struck by the thought that 'in privacy one may do as one chooses', but it is a freedom that has a terribly hollow ring to it. Not surprisingly, we learn soon afterwards that it is a freedom that doesn't really satisfy Peter Walsh, who, like so many of the characters in the novel, is torn between the 'freedom' of fantasy and privacy, and the need for real human contact:

He never knew what people thought. It became more and more difficult for him to concentrate. He became absorbed; he became busied with his own concerns; now surly, now gay; dependent on women, absent-minded, moody, less and less able (so he thought as he shaved) to understand why Clarissa couldn't simply find them a lodging and be nice to Daisy; introduce her. And then he could just – just do what? just haunt and hover (he was at the moment actually engaged in sorting out various keys, papers), swoop and taste, be alone, in short, sufficient to himself; and yet nobody of course was more dependent upon others . . .

(*MD* p. 174)

The 'freedom' that involves being cut off from the humanity of other people is not one that can give even the most dedicated individualist any lasting satisfaction. The contradictions in this passage – the desire to be alone and the recognition of his dependence upon others – are those of many characters in the novel, and cannot be resolved in a society which asserts human community at one level and stresses the need for competitiveness and individuality at another.

Clarissa loves walking in London, and thinks that 'it's better than walking in the country'. Peter Walsh, however, sees her most often in the country, not in London'. This disjunction is partly the result of the fact that Peter Walsh to some extent makes up the Clarissa he thinks of, but it also can be related to the fact that he remembers her in her youth, when she was associated with the countryside rather than the town. The implication that we are often left with by *Mrs. Dalloway* is that youth, associated with the countryside, is the time of human contact, while age, associated with the city, is the time of isolation. If this is the case, it is significant that Richard, according to Peter Walsh, 'would have been happier farming in Norfolk', a predilection which associates him with his daughter rather than with Clarissa:

> [Elizabeth] so much preferred being left alone to do what she liked in the country, but they would compare her to lilies, and she had to go to parties, and London was so dreary compared with being alone in the country with her father and the dogs.

> (*MD* p. 148)

It is true that Elizabeth here associates the country with being alone, but it is alone with her father and the dogs, enjoying some genuine human contact rather than the partial and artificial contact of the town. Throughout the novel dogs seem to be associated with the instinctive relationships possible in the countryside, and the howling of Elizabeth's dog during Clarissa's party stands as an indication of the limitations of the contact possible at the party, where, for Elizabeth, artificiality rather than naturalness and spontaneity seem to predominate. Both Sally and Clarissa think much of flowers, and the presence of flowers at the party – the flowers Clarissa sets off to purchase at the start of the novel – represents some attempt to bring this spontaneity to the party. But the flowers are 'cut'; like the possibilities of communion at the party they are doomed to be short-lived.

It has been suggested that there are moments when the group in a Virginia Woolf novel becomes like a single person, as, for example the crowd in *Mrs. Dalloway* watching the sky-writing aeroplane.[35] But surely at this point we are reminded more of the atomism of the crowd – each member of it solipsistically interpreting the message in different ways. There is an interesting quotation in *The Divided Self* which R. D. Laing gives as an example of the way the schizophrenic patient perceives other people. His patient comments that, 'In the street people come and go . . .' not talking of Michelangelo but just:

> . . . about their business. You seldom meet anyone who recognizes you; even if they do, it is just a nod and they pass on or at most you have a few minutes' chat. Nobody knows who you are. Everyone's engrossed in themselves. No one cares about you.

> (*DS* p. 55)

That inability to accept the familiar from which the schizophrenic suffers may have opened his eyes to something that perhaps no one ought to find normal.

# 6

# PARTY GOING

Leonard Woolf has stated that Virginia Woolf was always excited by the prospect of a party, although to this he adds the qualification that her attitude towards parties was by no means simple. It seems that Virginia Woolf was herself aware of the fact that there were contradictory – or at least complex – elements in her attitude towards parties, and there is a revealing passage in her diary where she seems to be trying to clear her thoughts on the subject:

> . . . my present reflection is that people have any number of states of consciousness: and I should like to investigate the party consciousness, the frock consciousness etc. The fashion world at the Becks – Mrs Garland was there superintending a display – is certainly one; where people secrete an envelope which connects them and protects them from others, like myself, who am outside the envelope, foreign bodies. These states are very difficult (obviously I grope for words) but I'm always coming back to it. The party consciousness, for example: Sybil's consciousness. You must not break it. It is something real. You must keep it up – conspire together. Still I cannot get at what I mean.
>
> (AWD p. 75)

In the margin next to this comment are the words, 'Second selves is what I mean'. These comments were written just after the completion of *Mrs. Dalloway*, whilst Virginia Woolf was writing some of the short stories now gathered together and published under the title of *Mrs. Dalloway's Party*. It seems obvious that to Virginia Woolf the party was a very potent event, and its symbolic importance in *Mrs. Dalloway* is underlined by the above extract. From her diary comment it can be seen that for her the party seemed to have a particular relevance to those questions of human communion and distinctness which occur almost obsessively throughout *Mrs. Dalloway*. The envelope secreted by people at a party (compare the famous 'semi-transparent envelope' of her 'Modern Fiction' essay) cuts them off from other people ('foreign bodies') and yet also connects them to other people, with whom they must 'conspire together' in order that the party be a success.

Although the diary passage presents the 'party consciousness' as one among several 'states of consciousness', its importance for Virginia Woolf would appear to lie in its representative qualities; it seems to present her with a heightened example of a number of basic problems concerned with the 'together-and-apartness' of human life. The envelope which, like the shell of the oyster, is secreted both to protect and define that which it covers, performs a dual rôle: it separates and communicates, connects the individual to others as well as protecting him or her from them. As R. D. Laing puts it, a firm sense of one's own autonomous identity is required in order that one may be related as one human being to another, and the secreted 'envelope' performs the function of defining this 'firm sense'. The rôle that Virginia Woolf ascribes to this envelope is very similar to the rôle ascribed to the hostess at a party, when she uses the hostess-party situation as an analogy for the reader-writer relationship, in which some convention is necessary before communication can take place. For Virginia Woolf then, the party is both a symbol of and an escape from the problems of everyday life, and it is in this dual rôle that its significance in *Mrs. Dalloway* must be considered.

The stories collected in *Mrs. Dalloway's Party* were written over a period of time during which *Mrs. Dalloway* was also composed. It would be unwise to assume too great a concord between the full-length novel and any of the short stories – just as it would be unwise to assume that the newly-married Dalloways of *The Voyage Out* are the 'same people' as the Clarissa and Richard of *Mrs. Dalloway*. To ask whether some or all of the short stories deal with the 'same' party as that with which *Mrs. Dalloway* concludes seems dangerously close to attempting to determine the numerical extent of Lady Macbeth's offspring. Virginia Woolf herself, in her 1928 *Introduction* to *Mrs. Dalloway*, said that she expected the novel to fly by itself once it had fluttered out of the nest and had left its mother occupied with a fresh brood. Nevertheless, a brief look at some of the short stories may help us to appreciate some of the significance that the party has in the novel.

In the story entitled 'Together and Apart', the following passage occurs, in which the 'envelope' defining the individual identity seems to have been burst through:

> Their eyes met; collided rather, for each felt that behind the eyes the secluded being, who sits in darkness while his shallow agile companion does all the tumbling and beckoning, and keeps the show going, suddenly stood erect; flung off his cloak; confronted the other.
>
> (*MDP* p. 53)

Here we see 'second selves' very clearly portrayed. The 'real' person is obscured and protected by a 'false self' who acts a part and 'keeps the show going', but who is shallow and secondary, and who is 'flung off' like a cloak at moments of real contact. The 'cloak' reminds us of the comment about the 'frock consciousness': an item of clothing, a 'shell' or false skin, is used to symbolise that 'front' behind which the real individual hides and through which he communicates to other people. It is of course traditional that special, 'nice' clothes are worn at a party, and these seem to symbolise the effort or conspiracy that people make at parties.

One of the short stories in the *Mrs. Dalloway's Party* collection is called 'The New Dress', and is concerned with an (unsuccessful) attempt to present herself in a new light at a party that a guest makes. Mabel Waring, the owner of the new dress, is not sure whether a party makes things 'either much more real, or much less real'. The reader is led to conclude that the effort she makes to change herself at the party only brings out more clearly those fundamental flaws of egotism from which she suffers. Clarissa, in *Mrs. Dalloway*, speculates along the same lines as Mabel Waring:

> Every time she gave a party she had this feeling of being something not herself, and that every one was unreal in one way; much more real in another. It was, she thought, partly their clothes, partly being taken out of their ordinary ways, partly the background; it was possible to say things you couldn't say anyhow else, things that needed an effort possible to go much deeper. But not for her; not yet anyhow
>
> (*MD* pp. 187, 188)

The party 'works' because, putting people in different 'envel-
opes' and in a different context, it is easier to come to terms
with the real identity that people have – the inner 'oyster'. But
the unreality of the party consists in the feeling that perhaps
the 'real', inner-person is not real, that our shells are the reality
and our inner-selves are merely our own fantasies about what
we are. The party thus focuses those central Woolfian questions: 'Who am I?, what am I?' Do we see people as they really
are at a party, or do we just see that people 'are' something different in different circumstances? Do we throw off the false
'cloak' at a party, or do we merely put on an untruthful yellow
dress?

Questions of the nature of one's 'real self' tend to be asked
only when it is, in a sense, too late. Just as the need to talk about
a relationship suggests that something has gone wrong with it,
so the felt need to work out 'who I am' suggests that some dissolution of identity has already taken place. Quentin Bell notes
in his biography of Virginia Woolf that

> Virginia . . . really more than half wanted to be invisible.
> The whole business of clothes was a nightmare to her; and
> she was happiest when she could forget that anyone looked
> at her.                               (*VWA B2* p. 137)

Of course, the person whose sense of self is very secure *does*
forget that anyone ever looks at him or her, doesn't worry
whether his or her clothes are appropriate. Mabel Waring, as
she leaves the party, tells Mrs Dalloway, her hostess, that she
has enjoyed herself whilst repeating to herself, 'Lies, lies, lies!'.
At the same time she symbolically puts 'the Chinese cloak she
had worn these twenty years' over her yellow dress. Mabel's
name – 'Waring' – suggests that her problem is that she merely
*wears* her new character, whilst preserving intact and unchall-
enged the unchanging and negative self. She wants to *be* the
same person as she has always been, whilst wearing a new, false
self that will change the way other people think of her and
behave to her.

Perhaps it is easier now to see in what way the party makes
things more real. Mabel Waring's yellow dress symbolises the
false, unreal self that the party calls into being, but because
this falseness is recognised, because her real nature stands

83

revealed, the party has at the same time made her 'more real'. Thus the party brings out Mabel Waring's egocentricity to the extent that it reduces her, and her perception of others, to disparate, inanimate objects:

> And what was still odder, this thing, this Mabel Waring, was separate, quite disconnected; and though Mrs Holman (the black button) was leaning forward and telling her how her eldest boy had strained his heart running, she could see her too, quite detached in the looking-glass, and it was impossible that the black dot, leaning forward, gesticulating, should make the yellow dot, sitting solitary, self-centred, feel what the black dot was feeling, yet they pretended.
>
> (*MDP* p. 62)

In the party with which *Mrs. Dalloway* culminates, however, it is Clarissa's ability to *give*, to be more interested in other people than in herself, that is exaggerated, brought to the surface, and revealed as her 'offering'. Unable to give herself to Peter Walsh or, fully, to Richard, she is still able to expose herself to the vulnerability of the party and thus, in some measure, to save herself from the fate of Septimus, a fate that her other retreats from commitment threaten her with.

I suppose that most people who have been to parties – not necessarily of the sort with which Virginia Woolf is concerned – have been struck by the extremes of fragmentation and communion that Virginia Woolf observed. There are times when people at parties, especially in their early stages, do seem to be reduced to the status of objects: separate, uncommunicating and awkward. There are other times when a genuinely relaxed feeling of communion emerges at parties, when people forget themselves but, in doing so, express their individuality in a socially appreciable way. The short stories of *Mrs. Dalloway's Party* stress the atomism and fragmentation of parties, whereas the party with which *Mrs. Dalloway* ends succeeds in breaking down this initial fragmentation and achieving a 'moment' of communion.

Virginia Woolf was certainly clear that the party was to be a crucial culminating episode in the novel; in one of her notebook comments, written on November 9, 1922, she wrote:

84

> All must finally bear up the party at the end; which expresses
> life in every variety & full of antic[ipa]tion; while S. dies.[36]

The variety that Virginia Woolf mentions here must be understood, I think, as the variety that includes extremes of human
isolation and communion; certainly one would look in vain
for *social* variety in the party with which the novel ends. The
party 'expresses life in every variety and full of anticipation',
it is used as a heightened example of the problems with which
the whole novel has been concerned, as well as offering a temporary escape from these problems. People at the party main-
tain a hold on their sense of identity and humanity but at the
same time move out into genuine contact with other people;
their separate selves are brought together through the action of
Clarissa, whose 'threads' hold all of them together, albeit temporarily. By the end of the party, after it has passed its awkward
stage when failure is still a possibility, no one asks, 'Who am I?';
instead characters perceive both their own and other people's
identities in an unusually clear and uncomplicated way:

> It is Clarissa, he said.
> For there she was.

The party is not just Clarissa's gift, it is the occasion for
communal giving, for that 'conspiracy' which will recharge the
participants' social sense and will allow them temporarily to
escape from their alienated selves. The reason why Ellie Henderson is treated so unsympathetically – both by Clarissa and,
the reader feels, by Virginia Woolf – is that she is concerned
only to take, to bear back a report, and not to give, to discharge
her part of a common responsibility:

> So, with her weak eyesight, Ellie Henderson craned rather
> forward, and it wasn't so much she who minded not having
> any one to talk to (she hardly knew anybody there), for she
> felt that they were all such interesting people to watch . . .
>
> (*MD* p. 186)

Early on in the party, a similar criticism is made, through
Clarissa, of Peter Walsh:

> Better anything, better brandish one's torch and hurl it
> to earth than taper and dwindle away like some Ellie

Henderson! It was extraordinary how Peter put her into these states just by coming and standing in a corner. He made her see herself; exaggerate. It was idiotic. But why did he come, then, merely to criticise? Why always take, never give? Why not risk one's one little point of view?

(*MD* p. 184)

Peter makes Clarissa see herself partly because he is so similar to her; his behaviour at the party early on is, ironically, similar to Clarissa's behaviour to him years before at Bourton, when she would not risk *her* one little point of view. But he also makes her see herself because when communication is inadequate then the individual *is* more aware of him or herself. In the act of giving to some collective experience the individual identity is expanded, regenerated and reformed, and thus the question 'Who am I?' is answered in practice through the self-confirmation that contact with others gives. It seems that the less we *think* of ourselves the more we can *be* ourselves.

At the very start of the novel Clarissa sees her party as a means to 'kindle and illuminate', and her rôle as hostess is presented as a specifically feminine rôle. Just as Clarissa cannot understand the nature of masculine passion, of Peter Walsh's love for her, so too she knows that her parties do not have the importance to Peter Walsh or to Richard that they have to her. Clarissa's rôle as hostess is aptly symbolised in her sewing – drawing together the folds of her dress with her needle – drawing people together at her party. Peter thinks of her as the perfect hostess, and there is a strong element of disparagement in his judgement. The basis for this negative attitude can perhaps be found in Peter's thoughts early on in the novel about the bell of St Margaret's, which is compared to the voice of a hostess:

Yet, though she is perfectly right, her voice, being the voice of the hostess, is reluctant to inflict its individuality.

(*MD* pp. 55, 56)

It is this submerging of the hostess's individuality that must precede the communion of the party that annoys Peter's masculine desire to assert individuality, to encourage the 'screen-making habit'. Yet, paradoxically, immediately after this

86

thought has passed through his mind, Peter has a clear image of the particularity of Clarissa:

> It is Clarissa herself, he thought, with a deep emotion, and an extraordinarily clear, yet puzzling, recollection of her . . .
>
> *(MD* p. 56)

Exactly the same movement from disapproval of Clarissa's renunciation of her individuality to a shockingly clear perception of this individuality takes place in the party. The implication would appear to be that one must lose oneself to gain oneself; renounce one's individuality in a concern for other people, so that in the act of concern for them one's individuality is perceived clearly by them. Being the perfect hostess is a gift for Clarissa in both senses of the word; it is a facility she possesses, but it is also a contribution, an offering, whereby she suppresses her egocentricity, her personal and private life, to contribute to something wider. Thus she speaks, as hostess, to Peter Walsh 'as if they had never met before', but this suppression of purely personal relationships allows a more general, non-exclusive and non-excluding contact to materialise – a feminine sense of communion which goes beyond the hard lines of the passionate, masculine relationship desired by Peter Walsh. To go to a party, people have to leave their rooms, and to make the party work they must forsake the separate rooms of their alienated identities and come together in a new, different, collective identity:

> Here was So-and-so in South Kensington; some one up in Bayswater; and somebody else, say, in Mayfair. And she felt quite continuously a sense of their existence; and she felt what a waste; and she felt what a pity; and she felt if only they could be brought together; so she did it. And it was an offering; to combine, to create; but to whom?
>
> An offering for the sake of offering, perhaps. Anyhow, it was her gift.
>
> *(MD* pp. 134, 135)

It is worth noting that the last eight pages of *Mrs. Dalloway* are concerned with Clarissa only from the point of view of other people's awareness of her; the last time we are 'inside' her consciousness is when she is alone, looking out of her window at the old lady. It is as if the movement of point of view in the novel reflects her loss of consciousness of self at the moment of success for the party.

Peter Walsh opening the blade of his pocket-knife, Clarissa drawing the folds of her dress together: the dividing and uniting tempers, the screen-making and screen-dismantling habits: the masculine and feminine natures as Virginia Woolf sees them. Both are necessary for life, but 'the screens are in the excess' and it is the task of women to repair the damage done by too much masculine division and compartmentalisation. Like Mrs Shandy, who, in spite of her sound common sense could never remember whether the earth turned round or stood still, although her philosophising husband had told her a thousand times, Clarissa 'muddled Armenians and Turks' and did not know what the equator was. This inability to come to terms with masculine divisions is, Virginia Woolf implies, something of a strength however. There are too many divisions in the world which separate people from one another, and it is the task of those endowed with that 'woman's gift' to attack this separateness:

> And here a shindy of brawling women, drunken women; here only a policeman and looming houses, high houses, domed houses, churches, parliaments, and the hoot of a steamer on the river, a hollow misty cry.

> (*MD* p. 181)

A world of separate objects, with policeman, church and parliament associating this atomism with the masculinity that Virginia Woolf connected with authority and the state. The passage continues:

> But it was her street, this, Clarissa's; cabs were rushing round the corner, like water round the piers of a bridge, drawn together, it seemed to him, because they bore people to her party, Clarissa's party.

> (*MD* p. 181)

The static and separate domes and hollows of the earlier part of the passage are replaced by the feminine waters of the latter part, drawn by the moon, uniting rather than separating, brought together by the party which symbolises Clarissa's 'lunar synthesis' of the separated 'So-and-so's' of South Kensington, Bayswater and Mayfair. At her party even the Prime Minister, no longer hidden behind blinds and screens in his enclosed motor-car, makes human contact with other people, and even Peter Walsh is taken outside of himself to a perception of Clarissa's separate yet related identity.

We are meant, then, to take the party in *Mrs. Dalloway* seriously. All must 'finally bear upon' it; it must express 'life in every variety and full of anticipation' – a symbol of that feminine gift for bringing people together, for reducing the 'screen-making habit', which will bring people into unalienated relationships and states of being. But is the party adequate to the symbolic weight put upon it in the novel? Irene Simon has suggested that it is not:

> . . . Clarissa's party is her solution to the mystery of isolated selves, an instance of communication, her offering. But assembling people in a drawing-room does sound a little trivial as an answer to the problem of life. Because the objective correlative is hardly adequate, the images which express some aspects of the theme fail to fuse, and the need is felt to establish the relations by means of other devices.[37]

There is obviously a sense in which any symbol can be made to appear inadequate by being considered in too literal a manner, and there is a hint of unfairness here in the slighting reference to 'assembling people in a drawing-room'. But this apart, the objection raises some central questions about the adequacy or inadequacy of Virginia Woolf's suggested solution to the problem of human isolation and alienation. My own feeling is that although *Mrs. Dalloway* presents and defines the problem in a strikingly impressive way, the reader is left with the feeling that the implied solutions are less than adequate. I would like, finally, to consider why this should be so.

# 7
## PRIVACY AND PROPERTY

I have already suggested that human alienation has to be seen as a historical phenomenon that has very specific social and economic roots, and that the contradiction between the co-operative production of wealth and its private ownership is its fundamental cause. We come to terms with other people by working with them; we are cut off from them by the private appropriation of the fruits of joint labour. It is in the process of collectively transforming external reality that man discovers both himself and other people. We may have any number of ideas about ourselves and about others, but it is when we work with them to do something that these ideas are tested and proved. I may think that that table is light, that you are weak and that I am lazy, but these hypotheses will be objectively verified only when *we* try to move the table. This is the basic truth expressed so concisely and economically by Marx in the *Theses on Feuerbach*. Marx sees the chief defect of all hitherto existing materialism to be the limitation of 'reality' to being an *object* of *contemplation*. The second thesis on Feuerbach criticises this limitation:

> The question whether objective truth can be attributed to human thinking is not a question of theory but is a *practical* question. In practice man must prove the truth, that is, the reality and power, the this-sidedness of his thinking. The dispute over the reality or non-reality of thinking which is isolated from practice is a purely *scholastic* question.

Perhaps even more relevant to our immediate purpose is his point in the ninth thesis on Feuerbach, that the highest point reached by contemplative (as against active) materialism, 'is the contemplation of *single individuals* in "civil society" ' (my emphasis).

Now in one sense it would be absurd to claim that Virginia Woolf was unaware of the importance either of material things or of work. Both as a writer and in other activities such as her work with The Hogarth Press her life was an astonishingly active one; Leonard Woolf's insistence on the sheer volume of her writings in his autobiography is a legitimate one. It is also undeniable that she was aware of the therapeutic and character-building effect that this work had on herself. An unpublished comment from one of her diaries, written around 1903, implies that she had learned to alleviate her sorrow through work.[38] But her view of such matters was, I would suggest, a partial one, and its partial nature is representative of the social and economic position that Virginia Woolf accepted throughout her life. In this respect, two comments taken from *A Room of One's Own* are extremely revealing. In the first, she quotes from Sir Arthur Quiller-Couch's *The Art of Writing*, and then adds her own comment to his:

> 'The poor poet has not in these days, nor has had for two hundred years, a dog's chance . . . a poor child in England has little more hope than had the son of an Athenian slave to be emancipated into that intellectual freedom of which great writings are born.' That is it. Intellectual freedom depends upon material things.
>
> *(AROOO* pp. 162, 163)

Winifred Holtby, in her book on Virginia Woolf, cites the above passage and comments that, 'Marx himself hardly put the materialistic interpretation of psychology more clearly'.[39] Certainly, her attack on the materialism of Bennett and Wells notwithstanding, Virginia Woolf knew that intellectual matters are dependent upon 'material things'. But another aspect of Marx's teaching, that the possession of unearned income, the existence of private property, prevents full and open human contact, was only partially understood by Virginia Woolf. The following quotation is also from *A Room of One's Own*, and in it Virginia Woolf compares the security of her existence after receiving a legacy of £500 a year from the death of her aunt with the bitterness of her life prior to this windfall:

> . . . my aunt died; and whenever I change a ten-shilling note a little of that rust and corrosion is rubbed off; fear and bitterness go. Indeed, I thought, slipping the silver into my purse, it is remarkable, remembering the bitterness of those

days, what a change of temper a fixed income will bring about. No force in the world can take from me my five hundred pounds. Food, house and clothing are mine for ever. Therefore not merely do effort and labour cease, but also hatred and bitterness. I need not hate any man; he cannot hurt me. I need not flatter any man; he has nothing to give me.

(*AROOO* p. 57)

Pausing only to wonder at the optimism that, in 1929, could believe no force in the world capable of taking away her £500 a year, we can see so very clearly the way in which what is known as 'economic independence' – that is, a power over the labour-power of others – cuts the possessor off from *human* relationships with other people.

Is it not because 'effort and labour cease', and because no man has anything to give her, that questions like 'Who am I?' and 'to whom?' start to assume a major importance? Isn't it, to put the matter crudely, work rather than parties which brings people together in a real sense, and is it not the case that a society in which the wealth produced by some is appropriated by others will always fail to achieve that communion so desperately sought by characters in *Mrs. Dalloway*? It is worth noting that Septimus too sees his alienation as a freedom at one point, 'a freedom which the attached can never know'. But the attached, it must be added, know a freedom which the alienated, in their turn, can never know.

Now it would be a serious mistake (although a common one) to fail to distinguish between criticism of idle, rich Clarissa, and criticism of far less rich, certainly not idle Virginia Woolf. It would also be a mistake to fail to come to terms with the fact that so long as creative writing is seen as an individual activity then the extent to which the writer can work with other people in the way in which a factory worker does is necessarily limited. What I am concerned to suggest at this point is that whilst being objective enough to be able to see what Clarissa lacks in her life, Virginia Woolf herself lacks the sort of experience and knowledge which would allow her to present solutions to Clarissa's problems more convincing and lasting than that of the party. It is arguable that Virginia Woolf's conception of 'life' is as incomplete as is, in a different way, Arnold Bennett's. It too often seems to involve the treatment of phenomena as distinct, complete in themselves, cut off from the human endeavour which has brought them into being. As Marx puts it, the life which man has conferred on objects is lost, and they become alien, separate from him.

> And so there began a soundless and exquisite passing to and fro through swing doors of aproned, white-capped maids, handmaidens not of necessity, but adepts in a mystery or grand deception practised by hostesses in Mayfair from one-thirty to two, when, with a wave of the hand, the traffic ceases, and there rises instead this profound illusion in the first place about the food – how it is not paid for; and then that the table spreads itself voluntarily with glass and silver, little mats, saucers of red fruit; films of brown cream mask turbot; in casseroles severed chickens swim; coloured, undomestic, the fire burns; and with the wine and the coffee (not paid for) rise jocund visions before musing eyes . . .
>
> (*MD* pp. 115, 116)

Both Peter Walsh and Richard Dalloway mention work – and in both cases feel the need to repeat the word so as to assure themselves, one feels, of its substantiality. But how hollow the word rings when they pronounce it! Is it not possible that Lucy, Agnes and Mrs Walker are nearer to a solution of the problem of human isolation than are those they work for? Nearer perhaps, but yet not there. Lucy has her work 'cut out for her', we learn on the first page of the novel, and the ambiguity of the phrase is decisive. Someone else is responsible for 'cutting out' – defining – what Lucy does, and so her work can be, again, only a partial discovery of human communion. Her work is, in the last resort, for someone else.

Georg Lukács has argued that in all great writing it is essential that characters be depicted in all-sided interdependence with each other and with their social existence, and he criticises 'Modernist' writing because in it the interaction of social forces remains unseen and characters 'act past one another'.[40] Now he is referring primarily to Joyce in this argument, but his objection has some bearing on *Mrs. Dalloway*. Certainly, one of the problems that many of the characters in the novel face is that they *do* seem to 'act past one another', and as Clarissa herself says,

> . . . how could they know each other? You met every day; then not for six months, or years. It was unsatisfactory, they agreed, how little one knew people.
>
> (*MD* p. 168)

If this 'acting past one another' is to be criticised, surely it is not a question of criticising the novelist's portrayal of it so much as of criticising the causes which lie behind it in life itself. *Mrs. Dalloway* can present the unsatisfactoriness of the situation, but includes no real solution to it. The critic William Troy, in a pioneer essay on Virginia Woolf's work, has argued that her writing was concerned mainly with one class of people whose experience was largely vicarious, whose contacts with actuality were incomplete, unsatisfactory or inhibited, and who rarely allowed themselves even the possibility of action.[41] The result, he suggests, is that 'experience' for her characters is an unsatisfactory thing because it involves no active impact of character upon reality. Clarissa does not know who her offering is for; she is, ultimately, without an aim other than that of finding an aim.

It seems to me that these reservations about the strength of Virginia Woolf's art are serious ones, and perhaps explain why it is that our admiration for *Mrs. Dalloway* is one that is hedged around with a number of reservations. We are led in this novel into the heart of the experience of human alienation, but we are not shown the way out, the way forward. By this I do not mean that Virginia Woolf fails to provide an adequate social or political analysis of the situation of her characters, but that potential sources of strength *in the novel* very often fail to be developed. The lack of the sort of alternative vantage point that the work of Peter Walsh – or Richard – or Lucy – might have provided, is not one that can be easily ignored in any final evaluation of the novel. As Dr Leavis put it, the envelope surrounding her dramatized sensibilities may have been 'semitransparent', '. . . but it seems to shut out all the ranges of experience accompanying those kinds of preoccupation, volitional and moral, with an external world which are not felt primarily as preoccupation with one's consciousness of it'.[42] The party is obviously intended to be an occasion where such kinds of non-self-regarding preoccupation with things outside oneself take place, but the reader may feel that the 'objective correlative' of the party is just not adequate to the task that the novel sets it to perform.

There is one lonely but important exception to the general criticisms of the lack of a satisfactory positive element in the novel that I have been making. Just before his suicide, Septimus is drawn out of his madness and makes real contact with Rezia in the process of their joint attempt to make a hat for Mrs Peters. For once, in this scene, characters in the novel are more interested in something outside themselves than in their consciousness of something outside themselves, and they make contact with each other by *working* together to achieve something outside themselves. The activity involves Rezia's job as a hat-maker, and we can note that activity with a needle is about the only practical work that Virginia Woolf consistently allows to her characters. The limitations of her social experience and vision are as apparent in this exception as they are in the absence of other productive work of an isolated or collective kind in her writing. But in this scene Rezia draws Septimus out of his madness and alienation through involving him in her work with a needle and thread just as, earlier, Clarissa had symbolically drawn the folds of her dress together with her needle. It is, initially, almost as if Rezia's ignoring of him to concentrate on her work allows Septimus to regain contact with her:

'Just now!' She said that with her Italian accent. She said that herself. He shaded his eyes so that he might see only a little of her face at a time, first the chin, then the nose, then the forehead, in case it were deformed, or had some terrible mark on it. But no, there she was, perfectly natural, sewing, with the pursed lips that women have, the set, the melancholy expression, when sewing.

(*MD* p 157)

'There she was.' As with Peter Walsh's perception of Clarissa's 'equivalent centre of self', as George Eliot expresses it in *Middlemarch*, Septimus's perception of Rezia 'there', saying

95

things 'herself', comes when the person whose identity is fully perceived is occupied in something *outside herself*. Just as Peter Walsh's admiration of Clarissa is at its highest extent when she is 'outside herself', being the 'perfect hostess' and making her gift, so Septimus can make contact with Rezia without fear when she too is 'perfectly natural', concentrating on sewing.

It seems to me that there is a rather simple point to make about these two instances, which is that for people of the social class to which most of Virginia Woolf's characters belong, the opportunity to be taken outside of oneself by work is not common. Is it not rather revealing that Virginia Woolf, in the passage quoted above, refers to, '. . . the pursed lips that women have, the melancholy expression, when sewing'? Surely that look that she describes is the look that any face, male or female, wears when its owner is concentrating on some task which involves undivided attention, and it is a measure of the limitations of Virginia Woolf's social experience that she should associate it particularly and (by implication) exclusively with women sewing.

Once Septimus has made this human contact, he can talk to Rezia. He talks to her not about himself, or herself, or their relationship, but about the hat, which he takes out of her hands and calls an 'organ grinder's monkey's hat'. The contact rejoices Rezia's heart, it is the closest they have been for weeks, and their closeness, paradoxically, involves both being taken out of themselves in the act of concern with something apart from them. They find each other and their relationship by forgetting both. It is because characters in *Mrs. Dalloway* are, too often, concerned with themselves, with their relationships, rather than with something outside themselves that demands their active, collaborative transformation, that the very thing they seek forever eludes them. It is noteworthy that Septimus and Rezia are not 'conscious of being conscious' of the hat; Septimus is just involved in the perceived separateness of Rezia's identity as revealed through her sewing, and Rezia moves from absorption in that sewing to rejoicing at the contact Septimus makes with her. Marx suggests that alienation is overcome when

The *senses* . . . become directly in their practice *theoreticians*. They relate themselves to the *thing* for the sake of the thing, but the thing itself is an *objective human* relation to itself and to man, and vice versa. Need or enjoyment have consequently lost their *egotistical* nature . . .

*(EPM* p. 139)

Now Marx here is describing a hypothetical state of affairs following the social transcendence of private property, but we can, in the contact that Rezia and Septimus make, see this sort of transcendence in embryo. Both lose their egocentricity in the *joint* activity of making the hat:

> What had she got in her work-box? She had ribbons and beads, tassels, artificial flowers. She tumbled them out on the table. He began putting odd colours together – for though he had no fingers, could not even do up a parcel, he had a wonderful eye, and often he was right, sometimes absurd, of course, but sometimes wonderfully right.
>
> 'She shall have a beautiful hat!' he murmured, taking up this and that, Rezia kneeling by his side, looking over his shoulder. Now it was finished – that is to say the design; she must stitch it together. But she must be very, very careful, he said, to keep it just as he had made it.

*(MD* p. 158)

The passage is so straightforward that it is easy to miss the fact that, in the context of *Mrs. Dalloway*, it is unique, for here thought and action, character and contemplation, are brought together. We are told, it is true, that in the midst of the party it made no difference to Mrs Walker whether there was one Prime Minister more or less among the guests, but we are not shown in any detail what *did* make a difference to her, are not shown her actively grappling with her duties as we are shown Rezia and Septimus thinking and doing the same thing. Clarissa is always *doing* something – going somewhere, buying something, sewing, crossing a street – yet whenever her thoughts are revealed to us they seem to be unconnected with whatever it is she is engaged in. As David Lodge puts it, 'We do not always think of eternity while serving potatoes; sometimes we just think of serving potatoes. Virginia Woolf's characters never

97

do'.[48] That 'never' is perhaps, in view of our consideration of
the hat-making scene in *Mrs. Dalloway*, somewhat of an ex-
aggeration, but not much of one. Of course, particular styles
have the effect, sometimes, of developing a momentum which
moulds the material they present; thus it is difficult for a
character in one of Browning's dramatic monologues to seem
other than talkative. But the disjunction between thought and
action in Virginia Woolf's fiction is no mere stylistic matter
– if there is such a thing as a 'mere' stylistic matter.

When the hat is finally completed, something qualitatively
unique in the whole novel has been portrayed, and, as a result,
a qualitatively unique form of human communion emerges
from it:

> It was wonderful. Never had he done anything which made
> him feel so proud. It was so real, it was so substantial, Mrs
> Peters' hat.
> 'Just look at it,' he said.
> Yes, it would always make her happy to see that hat. He
> had become himself then, he had laughed then. They had
> been alone together. Always she would like that hat.
>
> *(MD* p. 159)

The hat is, in fact, in many ways the most real and substantial
object in the whole novel, because, unlike the food at Lady
Bruton's lunch, it is not presented as if it is not paid for; its
cost in human effort is documented and, as a result, its human
significance emerges both for us and for Septimus and Rezia.
Septimus can become himself when he sees himself, and his
relationship with Rezia, *in something outside himself* – in the
hat.

In her essay 'The New Biography', published in 1927,
Virginia Woolf writes that

> Truth of fact and truth of fiction are incompatible; yet he
> [the biographer] is now more than ever urged to combine
> them. For it would seem that the life which is increasingly
> real to us is the fictitious life; it dwells in the personality
> rather than in the act.
>
> *(CE* 4 p. 234)

It is this separation of personality from act that characterises most effectively the alienated state of those who people Virginia Woolf's fiction in general, and *Mrs. Dalloway* in particular. Like Mr Ramsay in *To the Lighthouse*, Virginia Woolf's fundamental concern is really with, 'Subject and object and the nature of reality', and it is her inability to synthesise personality and act that prevents her exploring it beyond a certain point, the inability of a social class that sees its personalities to be separate from the acts of those who produce the wealth they live on. We can apply to Virginia Woolf the criticism that Marx, in his first thesis on Feuerbach, makes of 'all hitherto existing materialism', that it conceives of the 'thing'

> . . . only in the form of the *object* or of *contemplation*, but not as *human sensuous activity, practice* . . .

It is only for this brief moment during the hat-making scene that we are involved in 'human sensuous activity', in *practice* rather than disembodied contemplation, and for this brief moment the characters involved rise above their alienated condition.

This characteristic disjunction between thought and action cannot but affect the very texture of Virginia Woolf's language. A writer's language is not a neutral 'thing' which, like a handbag, can have any meaning the writer chooses stuffed into it. It is the accumulated richness of the life experience of that writer. A writer's language cannot give more than it has received, and one often feels that because no man has anything to give Virginia Woolf after the arrival of her £500 a year, her language has correspondingly less to give to any man – or woman. Her language certainly often seems to lack the evidence of having been developed through an active, communal impact on any stubborn reality. The relationship between words and things often seems to appear to her to be arbitrary, and in a sense it is because it is a relationship that has been forged by other people. David Lodge has picked up David Daiches's comments on her persistent use of such words as 'for' and 'one', as well as her liking for present particles of action ('crossing Victoria Street'), and has argued that there is more to these characteristics than Daiches allows for.[44] Daiches sees the use of 'one' as a means of indicating narrator-character agreement; of the use of 'for' as a linking technique to join different stages of association in a character's stream of consciousness; and of the use of present participles of action 'to allow the author to remind the reader of the character's position, without interrupting the thought stream'.

Lodge suggests that it is possible to go further, and to see Virginia Woolf's use of the pronoun 'one' as a characteristic upper-middle-class speech habit which 'slyly invokes authority from some undefined community of feeling and prejudice', and he suggests that she has not, for example, entirely resolved her attitude to characters like Mrs Dalloway, nor is she entirely open about the degree of indulgence she expects the reader to extend to them. Her use of 'for' may, he continues, suggest a logical connection where none exists, and the verb-participle construction can be seen to establish 'a divorce between cerebration and physical action'. These are serious points, and need to be taken into consideration along with the comments I have already made about Ann Banfield's analysis of her 'free indirect style' with its lack of an explicit speaker or narrator. Furthermore, William Troy's objection that the images that pass through her characters' minds are 'rarely seized from any *particular* background of concrete experience'[45] would seem to raise a number of associated issues.

Let us admit, to start with, that there are sometimes quite legitimate grounds for the use of some of the stylistic and linguistic features that have been seen by the critics I have mentioned as defects in Virginia Woolf's art. The second-hand nature of her images – their 'literary' quality – which William Troy brings out by pointing to the specificity and concreteness of the famous 'feathers' passage from *Wuthering Heights*, when the dying Cathy is looking through the feathers that spill from her pillow, is not inappropriate to the task of presenting a character like Septimus who, because he cannot feel, has no specific or concrete experiences to enrich his language. In his periods of madness Septimus becomes 'little more than a compilation of literary fragments from his voracious reading',[46] and it is arguable that far from being a weakness, this characteristic conveys his alienation and madness very effectively to the reader – as does a style which has no speaker or narrator. The question, however, is whether this appropriateness is more accidental than deliberate, whether, indeed, the novel demands some alternative linguistic (and thus social) vantage point, which would set off and 'place' the inadequacies that have been described. I would like now to look at a number of representative passages from the novel to try to ascertain whether or not the novel does suffer from an impoverishment which is either caused by or revealed through the impoverished nature of the language which is its medium of communication.

It is certainly correct to suggest that there are many appeals to the attitudes and prejudices of a particular social class in Virginia Woolf's language. Such appeals are notoriously difficult to isolate, although they are instantly recognisable to someone who lives in Britain and is a native English speaker. Accents do not 'come over' in print as they do in speech, but nevertheless there are assumptions, prejudices, attitudes and beliefs concealed within Virginia Woolf's language which the reader is invited to share and to confirm.

We can note that in *Mrs. Dalloway* Virginia Woolf uses certain simple distinctions of notation to convey different situations. When characters speak aloud their words are generally given inverted commas, when the words are those of internal cerebration they normally lack inverted commas. In like manner we find that when there is some implied narrator-interruption of a character's stream of thoughts Virginia Woolf tends to enclose such interruptions within parentheses. Thus an implied narrative authority is given to, among others, the following passage:

(June had drawn out every leaf on the trees. The mothers of Pimlico gave suck to their young. . . .)

(*MD* p. 9)

Like a number of other passages in the novel, the passage sees a group of people as an undifferentiated mass, within which individuality is of little or no account. But it also carries unmistakably suggestions that this lack of individuality is associated with the animality of those so lumped together. We do not normally refer to human beings giving suck nowadays (the Shorter Oxford gives the usage as archaic), and there is an unmistakable note of class condescension in the phrase, which can be seen clearly if it is compared to a passage which sees a group of men of the upper classes in a similarly undifferentiated way:

> Tall men, men of robust physique, well-dressed men with
> their tail-coats and their white slips and their hair raked
> back, who, for reasons difficult to discriminate, were stand-
> ing in the bow window of White's with their hands behind
> the tails of their coats. . . .
>
> (*MD* p. 21)

The uniformity of these men is seen almost as the effect of
conscious discipline, an impression which is compounded as
the passage develops further on and shows them standing
straighter as their (assumed) Sovereign passes, ready to attend
him, 'if need be, to the cannon's mouth, as their ancestors had
done before them'. The action of the mothers of Pimlico, on
the other hand, seems to be comparable to the emergence of
leaves on trees in June – purely automatic, attended with no
human choice or operation of the will.

It seems to me that in such congealed class attitudes in the
language of *Mrs. Dalloway* we see the same denial of selfhood
that the novel, on one level, seems concerned to attack. We
cannot imagine that Peter Walsh would ever say of a mother of
Pimlico that, 'There she was', although perhaps we can imagine
such an utterance from Richard Dalloway. What is curious is
that in the midst of a passage describing Richard's pleasure in
seeing whole families sprawling in the Green Park, immediately
before he smiles at the female vagrant, we have another distanc-
ing authorial interjection:

> (the grass of the park flushed and faded, lighting up the
> poor mothers of Westminster and their crawling babies, as
> if a yellow lamp were moved beneath).
>
> (*MD* p. 128)

Again there is this implied animality of the lower classes, who
are here seen as if they were insects gathering in a light.

At times we are given the impression that Virginia Woolf
feels her language to be somehow neutral, whilst the Edgar
J. Watkiss's of her novels, whose speech demands a special notation ('The Proime Minister's kyar') are in a different category.
The self-consciousness of this and other attempts to break into
the speech-habits and consciousnesses of people outside her

social world shows through in the actual language that is used. Let us consider another, longer example:

> That girl, thought Mrs Dempster (who saved crusts for the squirrels and often ate her lunch in Regent's Park), don't know a thing yet; and really it seemed to her better to be a little stout, a little slack, a little moderate in one's expectations. Percy drank. Well, better to have a son, thought Mrs. Dempster. She had had a hard time of it, and couldn't help smiling at a girl like that. You'll get married, for you're pretty enough, thought Mrs Dempster. Get married, she thought, and then you'll know. Oh, the cooks, and so on. Every man has his ways. But whether I'd have chosen quite like that if I could have known, thought Mrs Dempster, and could not help wishing to whisper a word to Maisie Johnson; to feel on the creased pouch of her worn old face the kiss of pity. For it's been a hard life, thought Mrs Dempster. What hadn't she given to it? Roses; figure; her feet too. (She drew the knobbed lumps beneath her skirt.)
>
> (*MD* p. 31)

There are long sections here where Virginia Woolf is obviously trying to convey the speech (and thus the thought) habits of Mrs Dempster, and her incomplete success is instructive. That 'don't know a thing yet' aims to convey a characteristic Cockney substitution of 'don't' for 'doesn't', and yet the effect of this is immediately neutralised a line or so later when we have a reference to '*one's* expectations' – a formulation that no one of Mrs Dempster's social class would ever use. 'She had had a hard time of it' recalls, perhaps, another characteristic working-class expression, but once again the effect is neutralised by another uncharacteristic speech habit – the use of the pluperfect – with which it is associated.

More than this, there is in this passage a very marked transition between the standpoint of the narrator and the standpoint of the character. This is the sort of transition that is normally impossible to detect when Virginia Woolf is dealing with a character like Clarissa, for whose mental and linguistic habits she has such a subtle feeling, but which jumps out of the page when she is dealing with a character such as Mrs Dempster. '. . . to feel on the creased pouch of her worn old face . . .' – this *must* be the narrator's voice, because not only would Mrs Dempster not reduce herself to an object in this way in her own thoughts, but even if she did she wouldn't use these words. There is none of the richness of working-class speech here, no linguistic evidence of that 'hard time' that Mrs Dempster has had, nor is there that ability to see in her as rich and complete a character as is seen in Clarissa. By the time that we get to the end of the passage Virginia Woolf seems to have become aware of this failure to get inside Mrs Dempster, so that the final comment on the 'knobbed lumps' of her feet is inserted parenthetically and give the status of an authorial interjection. The 'screens' here are in Virginia Woolf's language and social viewpoint which, whether she wants to do so or not, prevent her from making any real contact with a character such as Mrs Dempster.

Perhaps, not surprisingly, it is the characters who share her class viewpoint and linguistic habits with whom Virginia Woolf has most success, and this linguistic and social affinity cannot but suggest a deeper affinity between her authorial viewpoint and the viewpoint of her characters. This is surely why so many people have failed to detect her criticism of 'the despicableness of Ott' in her presentation. We need some alternative vantage point. In his poem 'Autumn on Nan-Yueh', William Empson describes the problems of teaching English literature without access to books, when he was with the exiled universities of Peking in 1937. He writes that remembering prose 'is quite a trouble', but that 'one tatter' of Mrs Woolf 'Many years have failed to smother'. He then quotes Peter Walsh's comment that (changing it to direct speech) 'Thank God I left that pernicious hubble-bubble if only to hear baboons chatter and coolies beat their wives'. It is not hard to see why this fragment should have stuck in his mind, for here we can see Virginia Woolf producing a phrase which, linguistically and psychologically, is just 'right' for Peter Walsh. In short, she understands Peter Walsh, is on his wave-length, knows people like him, and is able to reveal him through a characteristic expression that 'gives us' Peter Walsh both in his particularity and in his typicality. We learn more about him in that one short phrase than we learn about Mrs Dempster in the extended paragraph I have already quoted.

Perhaps this is one reason why few critics – myself included – feel able to give *Mrs. Dalloway* totally unstinting praise. We are given in the novel an extraordinarily powerful picture of men and women fighting a central inadequacy in their lives – the inadequacy of alienation – but we are shown no real way of escape from it. Thus, in the last resort life, alas, escapes.

In *Night and Day* Katharine Hilbery asks why there should be

> this perpetual disparity between the thought and the action, between the life of solitude and the life of society, this astonishing precipice on one side of which the soul was active and in broad daylight, on the other side of which it was contemplative and dark as night?
>
> (*NAD* p. 358)

In *Mrs. Dalloway*, as much as in *Night and Day*, we must give Virginia Woolf the credit for having asked the question and for having exposed one of the central issues of our time. That she was unable to answer the question she posed is no ground for belittling her achievement.

# NOTES

1. Blanche Gelfant, 'Love and Conversion in "Mrs Dalloway"', *Criticism* VIII, Summer 1966.
2. Everett Knight, *A Theory of the Classical Novel*, London, 1970.
3. Niels Bohr, 'Discussion with Einstein', *Atomic Physics and Human Knowledge*, reprinted New York, 1961.
4. Quoted by Charles G. Hoffmann, 'From Short Story to Novel: the Manuscript Revisions of Virginia Woolf's *Mrs. Dalloway*', *Modern Fiction Studies*, vol. 14, no. 2.
5. James Naremore, *The World Without a Self*, New Haven and London, 1973.
6. Ann Banfield, 'Narrative Style and the Grammar of Direct and Indirect Speech', *Foundations of Language*, vol. 10, no. 2.
7. Joan Bennett, *Virginia Woolf: Her Art as a Novelist*, Cambridge, 1964.
8. A point made by Arnold Kettle, *Mrs. Dalloway*, Milton Keynes, 1973. (This is unit 30 of the Open University course 'The Nineteenth-Century Novel and its Legacy'.)
9. Leon Edel, 'The Novel as Poem', *The Modern Psychological Novel*, New York, 1964.
10. Winifred Holtby, *Virginia Woolf*, London, 1932.
11. Bernard Blackstone, *Virginia Woolf a Commentary*, London, 1948.
12. Quoted by Charles G. Hoffmann, *op. cit.*
13. Quoted by Charles G. Hoffmann, *op. cit.*
14. A point made by Charles G. Hoffmann, *op. cit.*
15. A point made by Frank Baldanza in 'Clarissa Dalloway's "Party Consciousness"', *Modern Fiction Studies*, vol. 2, no. 1.
16. Boris Kuznetsov, *Einstein and Dostoyevsky*, translated by Vladimir Talmy, London, 1972.
17. John Bayley, *The Characters of Love*, reprinted London, 1968.
18. Blanche Gelfant, *op. cit.*
19. Shalom Rachman, 'Clarissa's Attic: Virginia Woolf's *Mrs. Dalloway* reconsidered', *Twentieth Century Literature*, vol. 18, no. 1. A similar position is advanced by Herbert Marder in *Feminism and Art*, Chicago and London, 1968.
20. A point made by Blanche Gelfant, *op. cit.*
21. Quoted by Wallace Hildick, 'In that Solitary Room', *Kenyon Review* 27, 1965.
22. In *Night and Day* we learn that much the same is true of Katharine Hilbery and Ralph Denham.
23. A point made by Jean M. Wyatt, '*Mrs. Dalloway*: Literary Allusion as Structural Metaphor', *PMLA*, vol. 88, no. 3.
24. Nigel Nicolson, *Portrait of a Marriage*, London, 1973.
25. A point made by Allen McLaurin, *op. cit.*
26. A point made by Jean M. Wyatt, *op. cit.*

27. Sylvia Plath's poem 'The Bee Meeting' ends with three questions which are left unpunctuated, and the effect is similar to that of the 'disembodied' questions in the extract from Virginia Woolf's Diary.
28. Raymond Williams, *The Country and the City*, London, 1973.
29. Raymond Williams, 'Literature and Rural Society', *The Listener*, 16 November, 1967.
30. Quoted by Charles G. Hoffmann, *op. cit.*
31. Dorothy Brewster, *Virginia Woolf's London*, London, 1959.
32. A point made by Jean M. Wyatt, *op. cit.*
33. A point suggested by Allen McLaurin, *op. cit.*
34. Virginia Woolf refers to '. . . Ann disappearing for ever into the dark London night', in her essay 'Impassioned Prose', reprinted in *Collected Essays*, vol. 1.
35. James Naremore, *op. cit.*
36. Quoted by Charles G. Hoffmann, *op. cit.*
37. Irene Simon, 'Some Aspects of Virginia Woolf's Imagery', *English Studies*, vol. 41, 1960.
38. Quoted by Nancy Topping Bazin, *Virginia Woolf and the Androgynous Vision*, New Brunswick, New Jersey, 1973.
39. Winifred Holtby, *op. cit.*
40. Georg Lukács, 'The Intellectual Physiognomy in Characterization', *Writer and Critic*, translated by Professor Arthur Kuhn, London, 1970.
41. William Troy, 'Virginia Woolf: The Novel of Sensibility', reprinted in *Literary Opinion in America*, edited by M. D. Zabel, revised edition, New York, 1951.
42. F. R. Leavis, 'After "To the Lighthouse"', *Scrutiny*, vol. 10, 1942.
43. David Lodge, *Language of Fiction*, London, 1966.
44. David Lodge, *op. cit*, and David Daiches, *Virginia Woolf*, revised edition, New York, 1973.
45. William Troy, *op. cit.*
46. Jean M. Wyatt, *op. cit.*

# BIBLIOGRAPHY

*Text*

*Mrs. Dalloway* was written by Virginia Woolf in the early 1920s and was first published by The Hogarth Press (which was started by Virginia and Leonard Woolf) in London in 1925. The standard edition is the current Hogarth Press one. The 'Modern Library' edition, published by Random House in New York in 1928, is worth consulting for the *Introduction* which Virginia Woolf wrote specially for this edition.

*Critical Works*

I have added a brief comment on the approach of the critic where this is not obvious from the title and where I have not referred to the critical work in previous pages.

Ann Banfield, 'Narrative Style and the Grammar of Direct and Indirect Speech', *Foundations of Language,* vol. 10, no. 2.

Nancy Topping Bazin, *Virginia Woolf and the Androgynous Vision* (Rutgers University Press, New Jersey), 1973.

Bernard Blackstone, *Virginia Woolf: A Commentary* (Harcourt Brace Jovanovich, New York), 1972.

M. C. Bradbrook, 'Notes on the Style of Mrs Woolf', *Scrutiny*, vol. 1, no. 1. (Contains some shrewd comments on Virginia Woolf's use of 'little asides' to deflate statements previously made and thus to give them a relative value only.)

Reuben A. Brower, *The Fields of Light* (Oxford University Press, New York), 1962. (Chapter 7, on key words and ideas in *Mrs. Dalloway*, has some interesting things to say on words such as 'solemn', 'plunge' and 'moment' in the novel.)

David Daiches, *Virginia Woolf* (New Directions, New York), revised edition 1973.

E. M. Forster, *Virginia Woolf* (New York), 1942. (Later reprinted in *Two Cheers for Democracy* (Penguin, Harmondsworth), 1970. (Harcourt Brace Jovanovich, New York.) This draws on Forster's acquaintance with Virginia Woolf, but has some shrewd things to say on the novels. It is in this piece that Forster points to the 'eating scenes' in the novels.)

Ralph Freedman, *The Lyrical Novel* (Princeton University Press), 1963. (Has a long section on Virginia Woolf which revolves around an impressive consideration of Virginia Woolf's attempt to combine subject and object – the 'inner' and the 'outer' – in the 'moment'.)

Blanche Gelfant, 'Love and Conversion in *Mrs. Dalloway*', *Criticism*, VIII, Summer 1966.

Jean Guiguet, *Virginia Woolf and her Works,* London 1966. (A critical study distinguished by thoroughness and intelligence rather than by a particular 'approach'.)

Charles G. Hoffmann, 'From Short Story to Novel: The Manuscript Revisions of Virginia Woolf's *Mrs. Dalloway*', *Modern Fiction Studies*, vol. 14, 1968.

Arnold Kettle, *Mrs. Dalloway*, Milton Keynes, 1973. (This is unit 30 of the Open University Course, 'The Nineteenth-Century Novel and its Legacy'. It contains some interesting cross-references to developments in painting parallel to those made by Virginia Woolf in the novel.)

Jacqueline Latham (editor), *Critics on Virginia Woolf* (Allen and Unwin, London), 1971. (A useful collection of extracts from books and articles.)

F. R. Leavis, 'After *To the Lighthouse*', *Scrutiny*, vol. 10, 1942. (Suggests that Virginia Woolf's vision, in its narrowness and indirectness, lacks moral interest and leads to 'something closely akin to a sophisticated aestheticism').

Allen McLaurin, *Virginia Woolf: The Echoes Enslaved* (Cambridge University Press), 1973. (Combines a sensitive and intelligent study of the novels with an investigation of Virginia Woolf's debt to the fine arts in general, and Roger Fry in particular.)

Herbert Marder, *Feminism and Art* (Chicago University Press), 1968. (Along with Nancy Topping Bazin's book mentioned above, this is the best study of Virginia Woolf's attitudes towards the nature of the two sexes and of her concern with androgyny.)

A. D. Moody, *Virginia Woolf* (Oliver and Boyd, Edinburgh), 1963. (A short but first-rate general study of the novels.)

James Naremore, *The World Without a Self* (Yale University Press, New Haven and London), 1973. (Stimulating study of Virginia Woolf's art as an attempt to reach 'a totally impersonal world', which investigates the loss of self that her novels present us with.)

Shalom Rachman, 'Clarissa's Attic: Virginia Woolf's *Mrs. Dalloway* reconsidered', *Twentieth Century Literature*, vol. 18, no. 1. (Sees Clarissa, whose true nature is lesbian, and Septimus, as imprisoned souls, 'prevented from free development and free expression by the society of which they are members'.)

Josephine O'Brien Schaefer, *The Three-fold Nature of Reality in the Novels of Virginia Woolf* (Mouton, London and the Hague), 1965. (To my mind the best critical work on the novels, which explores her 'vision of a three-fold reality composed of natural phenomena, social conventions, and individual experience'.)

Claire Sprague (editor), *Virginia Woolf: Twentieth-Century Views* (Prentice Hall, New Jersey), 1971. (A very useful collection of key critical articles.)

William Troy, 'Virginia Woolf: The Novel of Sensibility', reprinted in M. D. Zabel (editor), *Literary Opinion in America* (Peter Smith, New York), 1951, and in the *Twentieth-Century Views* collection, above. (An early but effective attack, which concentrates on Virginia Woolf's language.)

Jean M. Wyatt, '*Mrs. Dalloway*: Literary Allusion as Structural Metaphor', *PMLA*, vol. 88, no. 3. (Examines the novel's use of literary allusion to reinforce its underlying theme of continuity between past and present. Notes some significant changes of literary preference from youth to age on the part of such characters as Peter Walsh and Sally Seton.)